Ellis Peters'
SHROPSHIRE

Ellis Peters'
SHROPSHIRE

Photographs by ROY MORGAN

SUTTON PUBLISHING

First published under the title *Shropshire* in 1992 by
Alan Sutton Publishing Limited, an imprint of
Sutton Publishing Limited · Phoenix Mill
Thrupp · Stroud · Gloucestershire GL5 2BU

First published in paperback in 1994 by
Headline Book Publishing

This new edition published in 1999 by
Sutton Publishing Limited

A catalogue record for this book is available from the British
Library.

ISBN 0 7509 2148 X

 ^{TM} ALAN SUTTON^{TM} and SUTTON^{TM} are the
trade marks of Sutton Publishing Limited

Typeset in 13/16pt Perpetua.
Typesetting and origination by
Sutton Publishing Limited.
Printed in Great Britain by
The Guernsey Press Company,
Guernsey, Channel Islands.

CONTENTS

LIST OF PLATES

Between pages 122 & 123

Plate 1: Stokesay Castle
Plate 2: Bromfield – gatehouse to the old Prioy
Plate 3: Wenlock Priory, Much Wenlock
Plate 4: Shrewsbury Abbey with the refectory pulpit
      in the foreground
Plate 5: Lilleshall Abbey
Plate 6: Stretton Hills from the Longmynd
Plate 7: Ludlow Castle and the River Teme
Plate 8: Morton Corbet

INTRODUCTION

The shire is an artificial concept, thought up in every civilization by those who held sovereignty, to facilitate the maintenance of order, the administration of justice, and above all, the collection of revenues. Whether it is called county, hundred, department, (or even by extension, canton or province or state) it is an instrument of government, arbitrarily designated by those who have the rule to ensure that their household affairs work smoothly. The boundaries they ordain may follow contours and respect rivers and other natural features, or they may march roughshod over reason in some places, but time and use will gradually confer validity on what was originally a mere administrative contrivance.

It takes time. Only after generations of continuous and consenting habitation can the shire take shape as a genuine entity, capable of establishing a character of its own, even a distinctive language, and inspiring affection and a local patriotic fervour in its people. By the time they begin to boast of belonging to it, and concoct perversely derogatory jingles to underline their devotion, the shire is a formidable creation, not to be trifled with. Beware of taking at face value any such statement as

Shropshire born and Shropshire bred,
Strong in the arm and weak in the head,

even though I suspect there are several other counties that claim it. Beware, too, and this is an old pastime and an old occasion of battle, of shifting a single boundary stone that helps to mark the hereditary border. The passions aroused have not greatly changed since the Middle Ages.

Which goes far to show that it is not a good idea, after settled centuries, suddenly to meddle with the established arrangements, invent three or four new counties with synthetic names out of the mangled remnants of well-established old ones, and jettison one jealously defended shire altogether. County patriots do not relish being excised from existence overnight.

Shropshire escaped mutilation in the last revision of county boundaries, and remains one of the most entrenched and idiosyncratic of shires. Over the centuries a strong character has gradually developed, the very aspect of the land, the nature of the soil, its weather and prevailing wind, the quality of the light over folded hills and undulating fields, the seasonal rise and fall of its rivers, all combining to evoke a special savour and arouse a special loyalty in the people who have lived their lives there, and they in their turn have impressed upon their familiar places the mark of their own individuality, generation after generation. It is a two-way traffic between man and earth, even in these days of easy travel and sometimes enforced mobility. We have had to accept the necessity to follow work around, trailing our roots, but still the wrench remains painful, and the new surroundings alien.

'God gave all men all earth to love'

said Kipling

> But since our hearts are small,
> Ordained for each one spot should prove
> Beloved over all.

Now it is perfectly true that this one spot does not necessarily have to be where we were born. I can think of places in other counties, other countries, where I can imagine being happy every moment of the day and night. But none of them displaces this vague circle of earth, three miles or so in diameter, in which I have lived, or at least made my base, all my life. I can travel joyfully to any of my favourite haunts abroad, but only to this place can I come home. It can even be a love-hate relationship between us, but it is a powerful compulsion, strong enough to pull me back across the world from any earthly paradise. Other places can be where I exult and wonder. This is where I put my feet up and thank God.

What is the particular savour and character of Shropshire is hard to define. It used to be called one of the least spoiled counties of England. I am not sure if that still holds good since recent incursions, but I think it probably does. It is also one of the most feudal counties, in the sense that it has resident within its boundaries, on the lands held by their ancestors since Domesday, the greatest number of surviving landed families. Not so much a baronial as a knightly aristocracy, people who really lived among their tenants and dependents, and quite frequently in history did credit to the true aristocratic principle, which is the recognition of the responsibilities of status before its privileges. It is a marcher county, like its neighbours Herefordshire, Gloucestershire and Cheshire, but it is also an industrial county like its neighbours eastward. North-eastward it levels off gently into the Cheshire plain, and in the north has its own lake district and peatmosses. All its western reaches are manned by the border hills, upland heath still

known as forest though long ago partially
deforested, and now, in some places, being
replanted, and loftier summits reared defensively
towards Wales, many of them crowned by the
earthworks of early habitation. To the south it melts
into the softer, richer contours of Herefordshire
with its lovely, welcoming villages, and due east
touches the fringes of the midland conurbation and
the industrial and commercial tentacles of greater
Birmingham. Still largely agricultural, it
nevertheless gave birth in its time to the Industrial
Revolution, and sent out the apostles of progress to
the lowlands of Scotland and the valleys of south
Wales, and further still, into Europe as far as Russia,
to spread the word that iron was king, and
demonstrate the techniques to prove it.

A county of many contrasts, on the face of it, but
so is every county, yet still it resides firmly within
its own unmistakable nature. Within the many
strands that go to make up a shire there are no
contradictions, any more than among the
multifarious moods and tendencies that go to make
up a personality. Unity in diversity is what keeps
people fascinating, landscape ravishing, and life
irresistible.

ONE

NOT AN AUTOBIOGRAPHY

I am firmly resolved never to write an autobiography, and if possible to discourage anyone else from ever attempting a biography of me, but even a wandering memoir has to begin somewhere, and the best place is at the beginning.

I was born in a two-up, two-down terraced house, with a cellar, no electricity, no gas, a cold water tap in a washhouse across a brick yard, and an earth privy half-way up a long strip of garden behind the house. In front of the long row of diverse short terraces was half a mile of dead straight, dead level road known appropriately as the Flat, and on the other side of that a meadow that rose very slightly into a further field called the Long Leasow, topped at the distant end with an old pennystone mound planted with trees, mainly conifers but also some deciduous trees mixed in with them, a fairly open woodland which we knew as the Old Hag. I wonder now if even these names survive. My recollection of playing there suggests that at one time it had been coppiced, for there was plentiful undergrowth and a wide variety of wild flowers. The mature trees and established growth showed the age of the clay mound on which they flourished. It takes a good many years to clothe a spoilheap from old mining, and even lure back the nightingales. In our part of the county such very old workings, long beautified not by deliberate planting but by the wind, were common enough. Those slightly younger and less completely covered bred wild roses and great banks of brambles, and provided our blackberrying grounds in the autumn. Windborne seeds always lodged first in the slopes all round the mound – the flattened tops might stay under rough grass within the circle for many years – before bushes made their way inward.

I cannot claim that my birthplace was of any great importance. It was a small, straggling village half-way between the market town of Wellington and the valley complex of Coalbrookdale and Ironbridge on the Severn. It consisted of the row of houses along the Flat, where we lived, a further road of houses leading off towards the equally small village of Doseley, where our nearest Anglican church lay, and scattered dwellings in another direction, on the way to the little town of Dawley. A couple of general shops supplied our main needs;

one pub at the crossroads, another just along the road towards Wellington, and a third tucked away in a hollow on the way to church, a couple of chapels and a large ironworks, which employed most of the inhabitants from miles around, completed the amenities. The ironworks was then in the hands of the last of the great Quaker ironmaster families, survivors of the high period of the Industrial Revolution. Unhappily, it is now closed and silent, like so many of the magnificent but declining relics of the great expansion.

Considering all these evidences of an industrial explosion, even one more than a hundred years past and by now largely history, our surroundings were wholly rural. The spoilheaps had long since become woodland, the works pools haunts of wildfowl. We lived a village life. In my earliest years there were no service buses on our roads, and the railway station, on the line from Wellington to Much Wenlock, was a half-mile walk away. And walk we did, everywhere, and not only for want of public transport, but for pleasure also, having any amount of open, varied and beautiful country all round us.

I was the youngest of three, all of whom could read, write and reckon before we started school at five years old. There is nothing miraculous in this. We were articulate early because from birth we heard articulate and intelligent people around us, and easily became literate, without any conscious teaching at all, because my mother read to us, and with time understanding of the text from which she read seemed to come naturally, and out of that general understanding of words the more technical understanding of all the grammatical niceties involved gradually emerged of itself. Home entertainment such as hi-fi and television have more or less abolished family reading, I suppose, no doubt conferring alternative benefits, but certainly cancelling out that particular road to knowledge. We had also the inestimable advantage that my mother was artistic, musical, and interested in everything. She played the violin and sang, only in a family context, but her musical repertoire, gleaned from the cheap musical publications then already extinct but preserved from past years, ranged from folksong through music hall and Edwardian ballads, to grand opera, and as she sang all day about the house, we learned a great deal of music in childhood. She had a very sweet but small mezzo voice that changed very little in old age. I remember the only thing she ever bought on the instalment plan was a set of the *Children's Encyclopaedia* for us. I still have them. There were just eight volumes then, and the set is not dated. I suppose we got it about 1920. We also took *The Children's Newspaper* regularly, and our local post office had a little shop where we spent our weeky pennies, sometimes on sweets, but more often on reading matter. At that time there were two series of paperback-size publications called *Tales for Little People* and *Young Folks' Tales*, which for tuppence offered one long story and one short fairy story, with very attractive illustrations, just pencil drawings, almost as charming as the H.R. Millar illustrations to the occasional fairy stories for children in the old *Strand* magazines, which we also had, some in bound volumes, some in original monthlies. In fact, the house was full of books and music. Not very much else, but I don't remember ever feeling deprived.

My mother was the youngest of a big family, and several of her siblings lived locally. Her nearest brother, in Wellington, had also a large family, providing us with plenty of agreeable cousins. Almost the whole family played at least one instrument, some of them could get a tune out of almost any instrument you cared to hand them. The three miles to Wellington we often walked, and the three miles back, to see them, or to indulge in shopping a little more varied than in Dawley, which usually provided our day-to-day wants.

Being a Church of England family, we attended a C. of E. school in Dawley, generally referred to as 'the National'. The building was Victorian, with windows too high for the pupils to be distracted by peering out, and a block of lavatories across the yard. It had no central heating, but it did have fireplaces, and in winter fine hot fires, shielded by iron fireguards. Outside the actual schoolyard but part of the permitted playground was another spoilheap, still at the half-grassed half-bald stage, known as the Clay Mound and situated like a small open green in the other direction was the Grassy Mound. We needed a lot of space for the sort of games we played, which were frequently of the cops-and-robbers, cowboys-and-indians character, rather than the singing and choosing games that were still in use then, and possibly still are, in other terms and to other tunes. Other games came and went mysteriously in season. Everyone seemed to know, without benefit of diary, exactly when marbles went out and hoops came in, or skipping ropes, or the darkness games like the one variously known as Jack-Show-a-Lantern or Dickie-Show-a-Light, which required only one hare with the torch, and all the rest hounds in pursuit. When challenged, he who held the light had to switch on, and the hunt veered after the flash in full cry, and he was off again at speed into the dark. Naturally this needed a whole range of fields, and could be played only in the winter evenings. I won't guarantee that it never encroached into backyards and orchards when the hare was hard-pressed.

The mile walk between home and school we did four times a day during the term, for we came home at midday for dinner. Twenty minutes roughly to get home, twenty minutes to eat, twenty minutes to get back to school, it just fitted. There were no school dinners then. There was no time to linger on the road, except on the way home in the afternoon, or, if we started ten minutes early, on the way out in the morning. When opportunity did offer, there were attractions to be enjoyed. At one point the road ran for a long, straight stretch between the high wall of the ironworks and the pool that was its main reservoir, marking the course of the dam that retained the water. At the lower end of this stretch was the main gate into the works yard, and here rails crossed from the interior to run alongside the containing wall of the pool to the locomotive shed at the upper end. It was a full standard width line, but when only one wagon was needed it was drawn by two enormous shire horses, the very sight of which was a delight. The one I particularly remember – though they were very well matched – was ebony black and glossy as silk, as tall as a house and as broad as a barn, with great shoulders that could have put Atlas out of a job. Like most of his kind, he was as gentle as he was big and beautiful, and sometimes if we showed up at a fortunate time the old groom who looked after them would let us make awed advances to him, which he tolerated very graciously. But if ever he broke into a trot he shook the earth.

I also had a friend in the clerk in the time office, and often popped in there just to say hallo to him. Passing daily at the same times, we were familiar figures punctuating the day's work.

Opposite the works gate a narrow road turned off to skirt the side of the pool, where two terraces of houses looked out over the water. And at the turning there were two shops, the local Co-op and a small private shop beside it, the domain of J. Ball, Grocer and Sugar-Boiler, where my mother bought all her groceries. Mr Ball had a celebrated ancestor, the so-called Shropshire Giant, William Ball, or 'John Bull', who worked as a puddler at the ironworks forge. In his later years he weighed thirty-six stone, but was as famous for his great physical strength as for his girth. Our Mr Ball was of normal size, and a very kind-hearted soul, a good friend to families hard-pressed and forced temporarily into debt during the slump of the twenties.

Another attraction of this part of the journey was that the wall overhanging the pool was perforated here and there at the base, to allow the rail track to drain after rain, and in the right season new infant frogs came hopping ashore through these holes by the hundred, no bigger than a man's thumbnail, but perfect, lively and infinitely fascinating.

The pool was large, and did not often freeze over completely, but one winter it did, and remained frozen for several days, and in the evenings every village around emptied, and the ice was as crowded as a New Year ball.

Once, too, though I cannot recall the exact time of year, I remember seeing, from the bedroom window, having been awakened by the unusual light, the aurora borealis in full splendour. I saw it as a pair of translucent curtains drawn across the sky, perpetually stirring as if in a gentle but constant wind, and perpetually changing colour, very softly and subtly. I stood and watched it for a long time, until at last it began to fade. I have seen it once since then, but it was only a pale shadow by comparison with that first time. Or else, of course, everything was then brighter, more wonderful, more memorable. Yet the form it took I remember very clearly, maybe even the lustre was as I saw it.

In the course of the year there were certain perks attached to attending a church school, since we observed the major feasts and fasts of the Christian year, and at times that involved days when we went from school in procession to a church service during the morning, and were then turned loose to enjoy a half-day holiday. The pupils at the council school about half-a-mile distant were slightly aggrieved at not sharing these privileges, but otherwise they regarded themselves as superior beings, by reason of their more modern buildings and more spacious grounds. But, by and large, the rivalry was confined to the football field.

The church to which our school was attached was not the one we attended on Sundays. Ours was St Luke's at Dawley Parva, and even that was the best part of a mile from home. There were three possible ways to vary the walk, the least interesting being by the road. Alternatively we could set out that way, and then turn off through a valley of grass and bushes and brook called the Dingle; or, thirdly, we could set off in the opposite direction, turn down a lane from the Flat, and cross farm fields to another similar glen where there was a good, clear spring of water channelled into an outflow pipe called the Bath spout. These two more seductive ways sometimes proved so alluring that we did not actually reach Sunday school that day, but these occasions were rare. We did attend regularly, collected our text cards, decorated with flowers, and looked forward to the two great festivals of the Sunday School year: the annual summer treat, and the autumn concert.

The treat took place in the August holidays, and consisted of a tea and games and races in the neighbouring field, with trestle tables laid out in the sun – I never remember a wet day for the treat, but admittedly the wet ones are the ones the mind excises from memory. There were sweets and ices on which we could spend our pennies, but there was also Kent's pony, giving rides to the far hedge of the field and back, and all my pennies went on him. My progress in that line reached the point where I was allowed to take him there and back myself, instead of being led, but I never had the chance to get any further.

The concert was laid on for the benefit of parents and friends, to afford scope for our egos to expand and to raise Sunday School funds, every autumn, a programme of action songs, little sketches, even dances when we got ambitious, ending with a one-act sketch laid on by the teachers, who planned the programme and trained all of us willing show-offs competing for applause. Boys were hard to recruit for these duties, but the girls elbowed and schemed for position with a zest and low cunning that was good training for later life. Our school was remarkably well-equipped for that time, having a good hall, a stage, and two small rooms at the stage end well-adapted for dressing rooms. Times have changed. St Luke's church, made redundant some years back, is a dwelling now, and I have no idea what has become of the Sunday School building.

As a family we never went away on holiday, except occasionally to aunts or cousins for a visit. Few ordinary families did in the twenties; few could afford to. Consequently we made the very most of our own county, places easily reached that might well have been by-passed for years had those been the days of cheap flights to Spain and Yugoslavia, and well-paid work been a little easier to find. Besides all the adventure playgrounds we children cultivated for ourselves, in wilderness land like the old overgrown pit mounds and the deep wooded cleft of the Lum Hole running down to the river at Coalbrookdale, we did many things as a family. Sunday evenings, if fine, were given to long walks. My mother knew the names of virtually every wild flower, and the songs of most birds. We had no idea that we were being educated all the while, and probably neither had she any such deliberate aim, she was simply interested in everything.

All-day holidays took us further afield. There were a few regular, traditional days out. Easter Monday was for climbing the Wrekin, that single volcanic whaleback that stands out of the lowlands as the little mountain of Říp stands out of the Bohemian plain, as odd and as significant, and as wreathed in legends. The thing to do was have tea or ice-cream at the Wrekin Cottage, half-way up, where at that time there were swingboats as an additional attraction, and then complete the climb to squeeze through the chink in the crowning rocks known as the Needle's Eye.

In August there was the annual pilgrimage to Shrewsbury for the flower show, which diversified its attractions with tightrope walkers and other performers, excellent concerts by regimental bands, show-jumping and fireworks, in the beautiful surroundings of the Quarry and the Dingle, where for three days the great marquees blazed with colour and made the head swim with perfume. This trip we did by courtesy of the local pub, which hired a wagonette and horses for about a dozen of its regular patrons to make the journey in style. On arrival in Shrewsbury, before entering the showground, it was the done thing to call at Charlie Beddard's shop for one of his splendid family pork pies, every bit as famous as that 'Shrewsbury cake of Pailin's own make' celebrated in the Ingoldsby Legends, and then make haste to secure seats by the bandstand, from which forays could be made to the tents and the entertainments at will. The best bit was the journey home in the cool and twilight of the summer night, behind the gently jogging horses, with the last of the fireworks still coruscating in the sky over Shrewsbury behind us, and the moon rising before us. Luxury coaches know no such magic.

Being limited chiefly to our own county meant

that we got to know it very well. Towns, villages, museums, churches, mansions and ruins, railways and canals, all were grist to our mill. It always startles me when people ask about my research, since I am scarcely aware of ever having to do any, at least as far as Shropshire is concerned.

I have used this landscape, native and familiar to me, in all my books, sometimes in its veritable shape and by its own names, sometimes with its edges diffused into a topography between reality and dream, but just as recognizable, for those who know it as I do, as if it had been mapped with the precision of an Ordnance Survey sheet. I did not set out deliberately to make use of my origins. Shropshire is simply in my blood, and in the course of creation the blood gets into the ink, and sets in motion a heartbeat and a circulation that brings the land to life.

BLUE REMEMBERED HILLS

It is a curious and daunting thing that only in the most remote and solitary places, especially the summits of the least frequented hills, does man experience the awesome sense of being one in an immemorial succession of kinsmen, of his own tribal ancestors, a link in a chain going back far into prehistory, and forward far into the as yet unrevealed. Perhaps it is the same realization that caused sacred places in many civilizations to be set on mountain tops, and even inspired priesthoods to build mountains where God had provided none. The ziggurat, the Biblical 'high place' is a concept found in any number of lands, it must reflect a universal instinct.

To stand alone on top of any of the western hills of Shropshire is to look round on an apparently unpeopled world, and yet it is there that you may suddenly experience this conviction of having a place in a continuity of tenure of this earth that makes you securely one in a chain longer than history. It is not such a contradiction as it seems. There are always evidences around you to confirm what your blood tells you. Almost always, traces of the earthworks of very early occupation, when it was wisest to live on the hilltops, defensible places with open views against any hostile approach, safe above the level of flood, affording favourable look-outs for the prey the hunters needed to feed their families, and mass defence against such wild animals as might be a danger. It was only later, when agriculture and the taming of domestic animals began, that humanity came down from the hills in any numbers, to settle where crops would grow and there was fodder for their beasts.

Other evidences are there, too, of man's agility of mind and hand, flint for tools, the first workings to get metals from the earth, iron, lead, copper. Even after centuries the whitish spar of their waste, calcite and quartz, may show through and turn the earth pale. Where mining continued almost into modern centuries the waste tips glare, slow to weather and slower to grow grass and cover their nakedness. But on the summits you will not see this phenomenon, it lies lower down the slopes.

By and large, the River Severn divides the shire into western uplands and eastern plains, though a few isolated outcrops like Haughmond Hill, the

Wrekin and Lilleshall Hill do crop out defiantly on the lowland side of the river. All the west is high land. In the north-western corner, where a fair stretch of Offa's Dyke survives, the hills of Wales encroach between the rivers Ceiriog and Tanat. In the south-western corner – the two form brow and jutting chin of a head in profile, facing west, in the outline of the county – lies the great wild plateau of Clun Forest, half-denuded long ago, sheep country *par excellence*, home of the Cluns and the Kerry Hill breed, though Kerry Hill itself just breaks free into Wales. In both these regions place names tend to be at least as often Welsh as English, and most inhabitants have a foot either side of the border.

Within the shire, within the great sweep of the river that contains the uplands, the Shropshire hills tend to lie in diagonal formations from south-west to north-east, long ridges with escarpments facing westward, and eastward slopes declining gently into parallel valleys, threaded by pleasant rivers like the Corve and the Onny and the Rea. From south-west to north-east, spread like the fingers of a reaching hand, go, starting from the west: the Long Mountain – only the tip of it actually intruding into England, the Stiperstones, the Long Mynd, flagship of the Stretton fleet, the second flotilla of Ragleth, Caer Caradoc and the Lawley, and the great spearthrust of Wenlock Edge. In the south-eastern corner of the county this alignment tends to shift into the more compacted shape of the Clee Hills. Less haunted by folk-memory these, perhaps because they have only English neighbours, and slip unobtrusively away into the heart of England, even though the summit of Brown Clee is the highest point in the county.

The road which sets out from Shrewsbury for Montgomery follows the line of a Roman road, with unmistakable straight stretches, but at Westbury the original road leaves the present one, zigzagging to the right to straighten out again, just as relentlessly, at a high level on the lee flank of the Long Mountain. Here it is narrow, furrowed and ribboned with grass, but it persists; perhaps its first purpose was to convey legionaries, in the arrow-straight fashion of the Romans, from Uriconium to the camp at the Gaer, near to the ford of Montgomery, where at a later date English and Welsh used to meet to sort out their minor differences at law, and once, at least, to confirm a treaty of international importance. I traversed the Long Mountain several times when I was writing *The Heaven Tree*, on the way to that castle of Parfois which never was, and therefore could not be left in being at the end of the book. Once it was in winter, when the snow had thawed from lower levels, but on that lee slope still lay thick and untouched, so that we ploughed through drifts along the way, with the whole of that lofty world to ourselves.

The Stiperstones, for me, is the most awesome of all our hills, and the most unmistakably imbued with that sense of generations of human habitation, in a silence and a solitude. Even from the distance, sharp against the sky, its very outline, the long, stark ridge crowned by the jagged rocky outcrops of the Devil's Chair and Cranberry Rock, has a force and significance bordering on the sinister, yet in sunlight, with the sun stroking every fold of ground and sharpening every edge of rock, and the heather and gorse colouring the slopes, it has a variety and beauty impossible to resist. At various settlements in the folds of the ridge and its attendant hills the Romans found rich supplies of lead, at Snailbeach, The Gravels, The Bog, and Shelve hill, seams which could be worked from the surface in trenches. The signs are still there to be seen in these hillsides, and the mining went on long after the Romans were gone, until many seams were worked out, and richer deposits elsewhere proved easier to work and more profitable. The Stiperstones retains the impress of all those departed generations of labour and activity, pulsating in its present silence and loneliness.

Round such aloof and haunting places legends gather as naturally as cloud on the summits. The devil is always liable to take a hand, claiming all the best landmarks as well as all the best tunes, and there are several versions of how the most imposing outcrop of quartzite on the ridge came to be his chair. But he is not the only supernatural inhabitant. Like King Arthur and his knights in various locations under notable hills, like Saint Wenceslas and his chivalry under Blaník in Bohemia, a noble army of deliverance waits under the Stiperstones to come to the aid of the land at need, and rides out along the ridge to give warning when war threatens.

Wild Edric was real enough. So, possibly, was Arthur; so, certainly, was Saint Wenceslas, but in each case time and the racial imagination have made of them figures larger than life and more than human. Edric was a Saxon landowner of considerable consequence in Mercia, who in alliance with his own Mercian earl, Edwin, Earl Morcar of Northumbria, and the neighbouring Welsh, rose in determined rebellion against the Normans in 1067. Edwin, no hero, soon made his peace with King William, but Edric and his Welsh allies continued undaunted in revolt until 1070, by which time the king had eroded the opposition leader by leader, and finally Edric himself came to terms and submitted to the Conqueror. It is only fair that he should be remembered. Now he still waits under the hill for the day when he can throw out the Norman, and now and then emerges to ride the Stiperstones with his fairy wife Godda, on watch against any further invasion.

While the long crest stands open and jagged against the sky, the side valleys give shelter to abundant tree cover in a complex of beautiful and almost secret places laced with little racing brooks. The rivers of the plain meander without haste, lingering contentedly among their wide watermeadows. The streamlets of the hills plunge headlong until they lose their infant waters to one of the major systems that drain the county, and end, almost inevitably, in the Severn or the Teme.

On its eastern flank the Stiperstones declines gradually through a wealth of varied heathland and fields and plantation into the valley of the East Onny, flowing south to join its partner the West Onny not far from the southerly end of the next great ridge, the Long Mynd. Ten miles of it, the crest open and treeless, common grazing, its western escarpment very steep, and topped about midway by the hangars of the Midland Gliding Club. On a fine day their angular silver birds populate the sky almost as densely as visitors populate the ancient Portway on top of the ridge on bank holidays. In this sheer western face, for more than half its length, there are no valleys, for there are scarcely any streams to hollow them out, and only one narrow road ventures the laborious climb over the summit, and the even more hair-raising descent into the Carding Mill Valley on the other side, the most celebrated and most frequented of several beautiful hollows delving into the flanks of the ridge. On this eastern side the levels decline gradually into a complex world of winding brooks and folded hills, until the valley proper is reached. Down from the ridge in every fold of this complex flows a stream, gathering to itself lesser streams as it goes, and in the valley an almost imperceptible watershed mysteriously sends those from the northern end of the Mynd northwards to drain into the Cound Brook and the Severn, while the more southerly turn the opposite way and empty into the Quinny Brook, the Onny, and finally the Teme.

Along the valley itself are deployed the Strettons, All Stretton, Church Stretton, the main centre, and Little Stretton. The district is the home of a very good mineral water, bottled at All Stretton, and its excellent air and fine walking country make the whole area attractive to visitors. Fashions in recreation, fashions in health care, change with the times, and it is the active rather than the ailing who frequent the Long Mynd country now. The enthusiasts for gliding, hang-gliding, and walking throng to the heights any day in summer, but still from the summit, with its breathtaking views in both directions, anyone lingering alone can sense the centuries of human occupation, life after life, culminating in his own single person. The dead are there too, to bear witness. Along the ridge and among its attendant hills there are well over twenty Bronze Age burial tumuli, and any number of traces of earthworks, left as evidence of the lives of those who raised the mounds, and those who sleep under them.

The brook valleys that insinuate their way into the eastern flank of the Long Mynd are very beautiful, for the most part treeless except in their lower folds, but so suavely folded in their grassy slopes and so varied in their colouring and the play of light and shadow that they need no other enhancement. We used to go there from time to time as a family, before public transport and the proliferation of the car had made it populous, and the moment I remember most of all – the tiny things are always the most memorable – is finding, in the edge of the stream in the Carding Mill Valley, clumps of mimulus musk, monkey flower, with its gold and russet and amber colouring, and its velvety face.

We tend to think of the Stretton Hills as a homogeneous collective, but in fact the blunted cones that spring up along the eastern edge of the valley opposite the Long Mynd are very different. They are volcanic, like the Wrekin, and much older than the ridge of the Mynd. Ragleth Hill, Caer Caradoc and the Lawley march in single file towards the north-east, crests bare, flanks wooded in parts, enclosing lonely, sheltered places beyond, dipping gently through moorland into the rich, broad valley between the Long Mynd and Wenlock Edge. Once again the watershed lies innocently in the valley levels, near Longville in the Dale, where half the valley drains northwards, and half south, with barely a mile between the sources of the contributory streams, in what innocently pretends to be flat agricultural land.

There are seventeen miles of Wenlock Edge, and treed all the way, even clothing the sharp escarpment where the rock outcrops fall sheer. It is the narrowest of all these oblique pencil-strokes across Shropshire, and the straightest, but wonderfully varied throughout its course, and with splendid views over the rich valley to westward. It is virtually a double stroke, at least in its southern half, having a parallel and slightly higher ridge accompanying it like an echo, and between the two runs the intimate and lovely cleft of Hope Dale, delicately threaded by roads strictly one car wide, as if to protect its privacy. All the best secrets of Shropshire seem to be approached only by these high-hedged, narrow lanes, calculated to discourage wheeled traffic. Only drivers with nerves of steel take to them kindly, but they find the most delightful places by way of reward.

Beyond Wenlock Edge the wide, gracious expanse of Corvedale opens, farming country with pleasant villages, fine houses, fertile fields, but still from every road that threads the valley you are contemplating hills. Not long ridges here, but solid, compact thrusts of rock, the Clee Hills. Brown Clee presents the highest point in the county, but its neat shaping somehow disguises its height. Just once I saw it look like a mountain, when we crossed the Edge by Roman Bank from Rushbury, and from the crest, looking out over the deep descent into Corvedale, saw this majestic cone looming beyond in snow, burningly white and tall. Titterstone Clee shows a more dramatic outline, partly because of the extensive quarrying there, but it is not so high. From the road that crosses its shoulder from Ludlow to Kidderminster there are immense views southward, surely over three or four counties.

There are other hills, independent of the main complex, of course, red sandstone outcrops like those of Hawkestone, with their attendant Scots pines, the same stone providing spectacular road-cuttings round Bridgnorth; Lilleshall, of volcanic origin like the Wrekin; Haughmond, near Shrewsbury; Llanymynech, not far from Oswestry, where the Romans mined for copper, and indeed,

Old Oswestry itself, that immense Iron Age hill-fort, forty acres of it, enfolded within several rings of formidable earth ramparts. Almost every notable hill in the shire bears the marks of man's habitation and industry, his early fortifications building hill upon hill, his carving and burrowing for stone and metals seaming its sides with surface quarrying and the adits of mines. We change the very shape of the earth, not always for the better, and yet time and nature contrive to deal with every deformation, bandaging the scars patiently with turf and heather and bramble, and at the last with trees, even in the crevices of the rock, turning pit mounds to woodlands and industrial pools to haunts of wildfowl and water-lilies.

THREE

TOWNSCAPE

Shropshire is a county without cities. Its pride and glory is its market towns; more than market towns, indeed regional capitals drawing for their prosperity and character on the surrounding country over a wide area, rather than upon the town-dwellers themselves, providing services of admirable quality, and receiving in return the respect and the loyalty due from those they serve. Who needs London, when he lives within a few miles of Ludlow, or Bridgnorth, or Newport, or Shrewsbury?

It takes time for a town to develop character and individuality. Our towns, all but one, have had ample time. Telford is something that has happened in my lifetime to change the very concept of a Shropshire town, and it is a subject in itself, to be set apart and approached with caution. But all the rest of our main towns sit securely embedded in generations of history, shaped partly by the very fact of being in the Marches of Wales, where even stabilized towns could occasionally become Welsh overnight by conquest, and be reclaimed into England a few weeks later. While at the same time, and interrupted only briefly by these vicissitudes, trade went on between the two lands, and kinsman visited kinsman across the border.

Almost all of the principal towns were well established before the Domesday survey, and are recorded there with the names of previous Anglo-Saxon tenants. So are very many lesser villages and hamlets. Newport, it is true, was founded within the pre-existent borough of Edgmond, but as early as Henry I. The succession of names attached to one place, through the successive waves of invasion by which this country was peopled, demonstrates the antiquity of settlements such as Shrewsbury. The antiquaries, indeed, venture to fix an approximate date for the town's foundation as around AD 570, by the Britons, when the raiding of the Saxons drove them out of Uriconium, by that time deserted by the Romans, who had left Britain as part of Rome's withdrawal into twilight. But this highly desirable site, defensive within its loop of the Severn, almost an island and probably further protected by extensive marshes, had almost certainly been inhabited sporadically, if not continuously, for a long time previously. In succession it was Pengwern to the Britons, Scrobbesbyrig to the Saxons, Shrewsbury now to us, and it has been in its time the capital of the kingdom of Powis, when the Britons, hard-pressed to resist the Saxon invaders, moved westward, but for a time retained their town, the stronghold among the shrubs; the western outpost of the Earls of Mercia against the dispossessed native-born Cymry; the court of the Norman earl, capital of what was virtually an independent palatinate; and the chief commercial market not only for the shire, but for the whole of central Wales, in the more settled days of the eighteenth and nineteenth centuries. Such riches of experience and such diversity of use and population give power and personality to any town.

A peninsula in a great sweep of the river, with only one dry-shod approach and two bridges, east and west, to let people in and out, Shrewsbury was obviously an ideal spot for early occupation, and the addition of walls and gates and a castle bestriding the land entrance made it still simpler to keep control and fight off attack. So desirable a dwelling-place naturally attracted more and more inhabitants, and inevitably the enclosed hill-site expanded to the limits of its watery perimeter. In this century the advantages of Shrewsbury have become its major disadvantage and insoluble problem. There is simply no room within the town for further expansion; it has burst out for miles along the land approach, and even, with the erection of new large shopping complexes where ample space offered outside the loop of river, has made life precarious for some of those merchants who have their respected and valued shops within. For if there is no room for further building, there is certainly no room for the cars that carry the shoppers to and from the shops. They tend to go where parking space is available, choosing the sheer convenience, if reluctantly, rather than the struggle and vexation of reaching the old-established and intimate businesses they really prefer. Traffic is Shrewsbury's worst headache, and the struggle to accommodate even those cars that must enter has led to a succession of plans to free the flow by one-way systems, each one more confusing and infuriating than the one before.

Nevertheless, for all the obstacles in the way of getting there, and for all the regrettable things which have been done to the town in the hope of bettering the situation, it is well worth making the effort to penetrate the retired corners of Shrewsbury. It remains indomitably beautiful and surprising, in spite of the scars. At first sight largely medieval and Elizabethan to view, it has also a wealth of handsome Georgian houses, the kind usually to be found in regional capitals, where the equivalent of the London season drew the county families together into their town dwellings for their annual round of balls, concerts, salons and receptions. Often these eighteenth-century mansions hide behind high garden walls on the aristocratic rim of the town, looking out over the broad loop of the Severn.

I had occasion to be taken to visit Shrewsbury at regular intervals from about seven years old, having been born with what would now be diagnosed early as a lazy eye, but was then discovered rather late and treated simply with the prescription of glasses, which I have worn ever since. Since it meant a day out of school at intervals to attend at the Eye, Ear and Throat Hospital in Shrewsbury, and since my mother had transmitted to me her insatiable appetite for discovery and knowledge, naturally we gradually explored together every church, every museum, every alley and cobbled street within the town. Most of it she knew from long before, as she did every notable beauty spot or building within reach in the county at large. Shropshire born and bred, like her children, and rather late in marrying, by the time I was accompanying her on these jaunts she had visited on foot much more of the county than most natives reach now by car.

Shrewsbury is unmistakably a hill town – from every side steep streets climb to a noble and gracious skyline, the crowning glory of any town, here pointed skyward by the two tall spires of St

Mary's and St Alkmund's churches. A skyline that lifts first the eye on approaching, and then the heart, as the airy levels rear themselves terrace above terrace, another form of ziggurat and equally sacred — this is the first and foremost grand advantage any city can possess, to make it more memorable than its fellows. Vienna's street frontages (even to the shop names very often) are very like those of Prague, but Vienna is flat; Prague goes shouldering its way heavenward to the coronal of the Hradčany poised against the sky, with the spires and towers of Saint Vitus launched like arrows at the zenith. Paris is elegant, but apart from the hummock of Sacré Coeur it has no heights, unless you count the artificial skeleton spire of the Eiffel Tower; Athens rears its immense shoulders under the crown of the Acropolis. Edinburgh — well, where British cities are concerned, I can only say: Follow that!

Make no mistake, whichever psalmist wrote, 'I will lift up mine eyes unto the hills, from whence cometh my help. . . . ' knew what he was talking about. And in its lesser provincial way, Shrewsbury has this inestimable gift.

It also has a long and crowded history, both secular and ecclesiastical. When I was about fifteen I saw among the small ads in the local paper that someone in the south of the county was advertising for sale the two-volume set of the massive *History of Shrewsbury* by two scholarly nineteenth-century clerics, Owen and Blakeway. I acquired it for five pounds, surely the bargain of a lifetime. The methodical authors devoted the first volume to the secular history, the second to the ecclesiastical, going into immense detail concerning Shrewsbury's four parish churches within the loop of the river, and the two outside it. The parish bounds of some of them spilled over into the outer world, but even so four parishes centred all in so tightly enclosed a town present an unusual concentration of religious fervour. Times have changed. St Julian's is now a craft centre, and even St Mary's, the gem of them all, has been pronounced redundant. 'So patched outside, so beautiful within,' said Arthur Mee of St Mary's. What with the *Children's Encyclopaedia*, the *Children's Newspaper* and the County Books, I was brought up on Arthur Mee.

The oldest foundation among the churches of Shrewsbury is St Chad's, but not the St Chad's you will find in its rotund, classic elegance on the elevated terrace overlooking the great green riverside park called the Quarry, and the deep dell within it called the Dingle, blazing with flowers, which really was a quarry once. The original St Chad's has left behind a quiet relic pleasantly retired among trees, what was formerly the Lady chapel of a large, cruciform collegiate church with a central tower. The earliest church on the site was founded around the end of the eighth century, not long after St Chad, bishop and patron of the diocese of Lichfield, or more accurately of Mercia, is thought to have been recognized as one of the saintly communion. The last upon this same site came to an abrupt end in 1788, early in the summer. The north-west pier of the tower began to show ominous cracks. Owen and Blakeway tell the story at length; and call in a name later to awake many echoes in Shropshire:

. . . Mr Thomas Telford, then a resident in the town, was requested by them [the churchwardens], to survey the fabric and report his sentiments of its real state.

That gentleman, since so eminently distinguished as a civil engineer, reported, that in consequence of graves having been heedlessly made adjoining the foot of the north-western pillar beneath the tower, the main support of the steeple had shrunk, and that the whole north side of the nave was in a most dangerous state, which was greatly augmented by the nearly total decay of the chief timbers of the roof; insomuch that the weight was almost entirely supported by the lateral pressure of the walls, in themselves extremely defective; and that the least additional outward spread might bring down the ponderous roof with scarcely a moment's warning. He recommended, therefore, the immediate taking down of the tower, that the shattered pier might be rebuilt, that the decayed timbers of the roof should be renewed and the north-west wall of the nave secured. A vestry meeting, however, which was summoned on the occasion, decided that this alarming description was a gross exaggeration, and the suggestion of a stone-mason was fatally listened to, who proposed to cut away the lower parts of the infirm pier, and to underbuild it with free stone, without removing or even lessening the vast incumbent weight of the tower and bells. This infatuated advice was unanimously approved, the attempt was made, and on the second evening after the workmen had commenced their operations, the sexton, on entering the belfry to ring the bell previous to a funeral, perceived the floor covered with particles of mortar. On his attempting to raise the great bell, the tower shook, a shower of stones descended, and a cloud of dust arose. Trembling and in haste he descended into the church, and carried off the service books, and as much of the furniture as his alarm would allow him to collect.

The warnings were not heeded in time. The account continues with relish to the climax:

On the following morning, July 9th, 1788, just as the chimes struck four, the decayed pier gave way, the tower was instantly rent asunder, and the north side of it, with most of the east and west sides, falling on the roofs of the nave and transept, all that part of the venerable fabrick was precipitated with a tremendous crash.

Only three people even witnessed the fall at that hour in the morning; no one was injured or killed by it. The congregation of St Chad's counted its blessings fervently.

A very few evenings previous to the fall, the members of a ringing society had assembled in the tower to enjoy their favourite pastime, but as one of the number was wanting, the club, after waiting some time for his arrival, dispersed. An attempt to raise the ten bells would probably have shaken down the tower on their heads, and buried them all in its ruins. Even the slight vibration of the chime-barrel appears to have been the immediate cause of the fall.

The authors blame the parishioners thereafter for not considering the conservation of what was left of their church, but proceeding to demolish all but the Lady chapel, sole survivor now, and entering into the costly business of building a new church on a new site. The moral is drawn very firmly:

Thus the parishioners of St. Chad, first by neglecting the repairs of their church; next by preferring the suggestions of rashness and ignorance to the dictates of skill and experience; and lastly, by hastily destroying much that was by no means irretrievable, incurred a vast weight of expense, a third part of which judiciously employed in building upon the ancient foundations, would have given them a structure infinitely surpassing in solemnity and grandeur anything which has been or could be substituted in its place, and would have saved posterity from a burden, of the liquidation of which there is no prospect.

Owen and Blakeway are equally scathing about the eventual form which the new church on its terrace above the Quarry assumed. The architect was George Steuart who had recently built Lord Berwick's large classical house at Attingham. Mr Steuart wanted a circular church in the classical style, but the parish officials rejected such a novelty and insisted on an oblong plan with a spire. They had not reckoned with Mr Steuart. He was invited to present a sketch of a suitable plan for the alignment of a church on the terrace site, simply to be used with a map. So he did, but the church he sketched was round. However, they made no more of that, since the object of the immediate exercise was merely to settle precisely the best position on the ground.

When, however, the working drawings arrived from London, they exhibited, to the astonishment of the committee, the details of the circular plan; and to their remonstrances on this subject the architect replied, that by their desire he had produced a plan best suited to the intended new site, and no comment having been made on it, he conceived that it had been approved by them and he had accordingly proceeded to complete the necessary drawings and measurements; but he intimated his readiness to prepare a new set of drawings, on being paid for those which he had understood them to adopt . . .

They gave in. New St Chad's is a circular church, 100 feet in diameter, with a belfry and cupola. 'An ill-proportioned cross and vane,' says the history sourly, 'crowns the whole'. However, it does admit somewhat grudgingly, 'The whole interior is handsome'.

I suspect that New St Chad's is still a divisive subject, much liked or much disliked. In its day it must have been revolutionary in the eyes of the people of Shrewsbury. Since my own fancy is for the particularly English Early English of around 1220, when the stiff leaf capitals of *The Heaven Tree* held up the pillars of the earth, I naturally incline to St Mary's. But externally it seems to me that St Chad's fills its position above the Quarry and the river with a certain grace.

The second saint to have a church dedicated to him in Shrewsbury was St Alkmund, around the year 900, possibly by Ethelfleda, Alfred's formidable daughter, the Lady of the Mercians. Again what you see is far from what you would have seen prior to the fall of Old St Chad's, a disaster which seems to have frightened the people of the neighbouring parish into a hurried examination of their own church. The building was cruciform, so Owen and Blakeway tell us, and had developed gradually with features ranging from Anglo-Norman to sixteenth century. Though they found very little amiss with its stability, and nothing that could not easily and economically have been put right, they were so disturbed that they decided to demolish it and build again on a similar scale. Of the desecration of the interior during demolition the history says with quite justifiable horror: '*The Brasses were sold by weight*, and the gravestones dispersed and converted to common uses!'

But they kept the tower and steeple, 'more, probably, from the deficiency of funds for the erection of a new one, than from a sense of its uncommon beauty.' Owen and Blakeway did not approve of much that had been done to Shrewsbury even in their day. I wonder what they would say of developments now!

From the past of the old St Alkmund's the history quotes an unnamed Chronicler:

> Upon Twelfth Day, 1553, the dyvyll appeared in Saint Alkmond's church when the preest was at Highe Masse, with great tempest and darckeness, so that as he passyd through the churche he mountyd up the steeple, Terynge the wyer of the clocke, and put the prynt of his clawes uppon the fourth bell, and toocke one of the pynnacles awaye with hym, and for the tyme stayed all the bells in the churches within the towne that they could neyther toll nor rynge.

Storms must have swept the whole country that day, for similar reports arise in other parts of England, with almost every one put down to the devil's account.

St Julian's foundation also goes back to Saxon times, but whatever fabric existed up to 1748 had become ruinous, and it suffered the same fate of demolition, all but the tower, and was replaced by a plain oblong of red brick, sitting cheek by jowl with St Alkmund's. It is a craft centre now, with a dwelling in the tower, an enviable place to live, I should think, in one of the most pleasant corners of the town, the gracious, enclosed green of St Alkmund's Place.

But it is a genuine grief that St Mary's, the lovely survivor, 'so patched outside, so beautiful within', should cease to be a place of worship, being itself so worshipful. What is to become of it no one can say. I hope, something worthy. For St Mary's has not been spoiled. Additions were made to it early in the thirteenth century, when it was extended into aisles, and it was then it acquired the splendid stiff-leaf capitals of the grouped pillars in the arcades.

Over the centuries, of course, minor things have been done to it, but always harmoniously. And in the nineteenth century, thanks to the efforts of a discerning incumbent, it gained its splendour of fifteenth- and sixteenth-century Flemish and German glass, a wonderful collection picked up in Cologne and Trier and the Netherlands, some by the vicar, Mr Rowland, some handed on to his care and use by Sir Brooke Boothby, of Ashbourne in Derbyshire, who had also given to Lichfield cathedral the glorious glass now in the Lady chapel, where Mr Rowland arranged its installation. There is a whole window of scenes from the life of Saint Bernard, finely drawn in grisaille, as well as much resplendent colour. But the chief treasure is not continental, but early English work, the great Jesse window showing the descent of Christ through the line of David. Probably it was made locally. I like to think so. It has had some miraculous escapes, for it survived the collapse of St Chad's, from which church it was brought here to St Mary's.

Outside the ring of the Severn lies the Abbey church of St Peter and St Paul, the creation of the Norman earl, Roger de Montgomery, who built and endowed the stone monastic foundation at the prompting of his counsellor and chaplain Odelerius, who was already patron of the wooden church on the site. The monastery suffered the fate of all its kind at the Dissolution, the land and property were sold off, the buildings turned into a convenient quarry for ready-cut stone, and the leavings abandoned to decay. But the church, being also the parish church of Holy Cross, survived, shorn of its east end and Lady chapel, and with the scars of the cloister walls seaming its sides. The nave is still massive Norman work, with thick columns and round arches. The east end is Victorian, the work of John Loughborough Pearson, about 1886, since the non-parochial part of the church was barbarously ripped off, along with everything that called to mind a monastic house. But I find Pearson's chancel very fine, austere, dignified, even beautiful.

The abbey has meant a great deal to me since I was drawn more closely into its affairs, in its nine hundredth year, 1983, by my dear friend

Prebendary Ralph Lumley, then vicar. The little, worn shrine of St Winifred in the abbey gave rise to the very existence of Brother Cadfael, imaginary monk of a very real Benedictine house. I hope that the former abbey grounds may yet be reunited with the church itself, and grow into a significant and worthy centre of interest to visitors, and a source of pride to the inhabitants.

Shrewsbury also housed three friaries, the Dominicans close to the river by St Mary's Water Lane, under the slope of what was once the abbot's vineyard, the Austin friars to the west, at the bottom of modern Barker Street, and the Franciscans to the south-east; all of them outside the walls and close to the Severn. The friars came too late to find a location within the walled town. The name of Greyfriars keeps the Franciscans in memory, and only of their house does any noticeable trace remain, in the stonework, windows and doors of some later cottages.

At the end of the Abbey Foregate, where the roads divide, lies the church of St Giles, to all appearances modestly Victorian, as indeed most of its fabric is; but within, the memory of the original church of the medieval leper hospital is strongly present, for the nave is Norman, the font is Norman, and some other traces remain from slightly later times to keep its long and honourable history in mind.

Roger de Montgomery's castle, built originally to protect the only dry-shod approach to the town, has passed through many changes and additions since its inception, but still has its general shape after the attentions of a host of builders and architects from Edward I to Thomas Telford, and can show an unmistakably Norman gateway; and the mass of the great hall, after much alteration, is still basically as Edward I left it. There are other public buildings to be visited: the old Grammar School where the inseparables Philip Sidney and Fulke Greville were educated, now become the town library and museum, after the school outgrew its origins, and moved to the lofty ridge of Kingsland, across the river from the Quarry; the late sixteenth-century Market Hall in the square; the Council House gateway; the museum of Roman Antiquities from Uriconium, housed in Rowley's Mansion, the magnificent house of a Jacobean brewer, and the greatest of the merchant houses of Shrewsbury. And of course, the bridges, the two ancient guarded ways into the town, one from England, one from Wales. The Welsh bridge has lost the tower that spanned it until the mid-eighteenth century; an engraving of 1732 shows it still commanding the passage, a pointed archway with a crenellated crest, flanked by two rounded corner towers, with a stone figure of a man in armour mounted above the gate.

This gentleman, now installed above the Old Market Hall in the square, is thought to be Richard Plantagenet, Duke of York, the unfortunate aspirant to the throne who was killed at the battle of Wakefield, and who fathered Edward IV and Richard III. Shrewsbury was strongly attached to the Yorkist cause in the Wars of the Roses, though it baulked at endorsing Richard's tenure when it had a choice, and a substantial part of the Shropshire gentry declared for Henry Tudor on his way through this town to the field of Bosworth. There are other bridges now, the Castle Bridge, Kingsland Bridge, Porthill Bridge, Greyfriars Bridge — footbridges, some of them, a whole bracelet of bridges. It is no longer essential to maintain a check on every soul who goes in and out, as it once was.

But the real distinction of Shrewsbury is not in individual buildings, splendid though they may be, but in its streetscapes, whole harmonious rows of fine black and white frontages, tall, gabled, ranging from the earlier simple and elegant stripes to the complex herring-boning and diapering of later elaborations. These were the town houses of wealthy merchant families in the high period of the sixteenth and seventeenth centuries, before the equally fine Georgians came in with the eighteenth century. Like Rowley's house elsewhere, Ireland's Mansion, Owen's Mansion, Lloyd's Mansion, all in

High Street, still bear the names of the families that founded them. St Mary's Place has Drapers' Hall, the home of the guild. The guilds were strong here, as in most provincial capitals, and left names that speak for themselves. Butchers' Row is exactly what it claims to be, a whole street of sixteenth-century shop-fronts in elegant harmony. Next in the hierarchy of the streets come more devious, narrow, winding lanes, some still cobbled, overhung by leaning Elizabethan storeys braced on enormous beams; Fish Street and Milk Street, trade names once again, steep and curving as they go; and shyest and most secret of all, the 'shuts' of Shrewsbury, passages that slip between the buildings and offer short cuts everywhere, some sheltering old inns, some still lined with small specialist shops.

Most of these highways and byways, from the greatest to the most secretive, bear unusual and charming names which avoid the very mention of the word 'street': Shoplatch, Murivance, Belmont, Claremont, Mardol, Bellstone, Grope Lane, Wyle Cop, Gullet Passage, Golden Cross Passage, Town Walls, Dogpole, Abbey Foregate and Castle Foregate. Streets are the exception. The word is redundant, as the true Salopian may well bristle when the unenlightened speak (as they sometimes do!) of the Quarry Park. Their green bowl running down to the Severn, the prospect of the school on its fellow green eminence, and the boathouses opposite, is simply the Quarry.

Fully equal in dignity and beauty, Ludlow, the county's southern capital and social centre, has the advantage over Shrewsbury in one important particular: it now possesses a new and effective bypass, and is spared the horror of heavy vehicles blundering brutally through its gracious streets.

Ludlow is the model of an Anglo-Norman town planted under the aegis of either castle or monastic foundation. In this case a castle, the central pivot of the entire line of border fortresses that monitor the Welsh border from Chepstow to Chester. By the same token, it is again a hill town, to afford the garrison and castellan a firmly defensible field. And again it is partially encircled by two rivers conjoining at its north-western corner. There the Corve flows into the Teme, and the augmented waters flow round the western side and round to the south, leaving only the side towards England without its moat. The short, bold ridge of which the castle occupies the western end rears 200 feet at that point from the Teme, in a treed slope beneath the castle walls. On this ridge the town began unfolding, first establishing the other two of the three essential elements for a successful castle town, the market and the church. The church stands at the eastern end of the ridge, and originally the marketplace stretched the whole way between, in ample width to accommodate the stalls of a thriving commerce. But later this imposing street became instead a maze of narrow lanes, as enterprising stallholders built themselves permanent shops to replace their movable booths, colonizing the whole generous space. From Castle Square you now approach the church by narrow, intriguing passages crowded with fascinating shops, to emerge into a quiet green enclosing the finest parish church in the county, and looking out over the town wall upon an expanse of rich green fields and the meanderings of Corve and Teme as they draw together and embrace.

The town thrived, first as a defensive stronghold containing the Welsh threat, and a well-placed centre of trade, later as an administrative power when the Council of the Marches was based there, and the castle became royal. So it expanded in the logical direction, and by planned and orderly stages, gradually downhill into England, into the lowlands. Southward it grew to the riverside, and cast a narrow bridge across the Teme into the equally old hamlet of Ludford.

Down from the ridge to this humped and narrow bridge plunges a magnificent street, straight as an arrow, lined with medieval frontages at its upper end, and tracing its way through the centuries as it goes, by way of the splendid town houses of the eighteenth-century county familes, to shrink abruptly to a quarter of its width, and stoop to pass through the Broad Gate, last of the seven gates of the old town, topped by a castellated eighteenth-century house. Beyond, Lower Broad Street expands again into its paved and cobbled pride, and continues to the bridge.

Parallel with Broad Street to westward, and almost as splendid, goes Mill Street. Move outward from Ludlow's centre in any direction, and you are moving through the ages towards today. Latecomers hang upon the fringes, the crest is already taken, very long ago.

And the two particular dominants, church and castle, would be hard to match anywhere. Ludlow does nothing by halves. The church of St Laurence is very large, the tower is very tall. It dates back to the end of the twelfth century, but most of what you see now belongs to the fourteenth and fifteenth. Tall nave, wide aisles, splendid stained glass, in part surely local, and with lavish use of the special soft shade known as Ludlow blue, another Tree of Jesse window, but this one with some nineteenth-century restoration. And rich in the blue, the Palmers' window, recounting a legend of Edward the Confessor and the pilgrims to Jerusalem. The Palmers had a strong guild in Ludlow. Indeed,

Ludlow's history is concerned as much with strong merchant guilds and wealthy wool merchants as it is with kings and wars and long-past tragedies, and it has plenty of those.

The poppyheads and misericords of the chancel are famous. The latter in particular afforded the craftsman scope to indulge his fancy, his humour, and often his irreverence, and this collection is among the finest anywhere.

Of black and white pubs, Ludlow has a wealth, besides the one everyone knows from photographs, the celebrated Feathers Hotel, with its triple gable, projecting storeys, first floor balcony, and prodigy of black and white patterning. The Old Bull on the Bull Ring is just as fine in its own way, the Angel not too far behind. Both the Old Bull and the Feathers are as notable within as without. And everywhere the domestic and social architecture of the town, from the Reader's House in the church close, with its medieval stone ground floor and its three-storey black and white porch, and Castle Lodge on the corner of Mill Street, similarly stone below and black and white above, to the gateway of what was once the Carmelite foundation here, and the fifteenth-century Guildhall of the Palmers' Guild, is well worth noticing.

The castle, overhanging the steep slope to the Teme, the weir, and Dinham Bridge, presents a long curtain wall to westward, much of it still twelfth century. The view from the river below, and the bridge, is formidable and beautiful, the weir a lavish extra adornment. But the best views of both castle and town are from the lofty ridge of the Whitcliffe opposite, a noble panorama of one of the most perfect towns in Britain, changing and unfolding as you walk the terraced road, and enhanced at every change.

At close quarters the castle loses nothing of its distinction. Its outer bailey is the biggest open space in Ludlow. Two whole ranges of mainly Elizabethan buildings along the inner side of its eastern and southern walls hardly diminish it. Across a deep moat and through the enormous gatehouse-keep you enter the inner bailey and face the long range of the main living quarters, with the great hall in which Lawes conducted the first performance of Milton's *Comus*, with Milton himself present. It was written for the Earl of Bridgewater and his family when he became Lord President of the Council of the Marches, and the Lady in the masque was a delicate compliment to the Lord President's daughter.

I don't recall the year, though it was a very long time ago, when the Ludlow Festival was first mooted — or was it revived after a long interval? I can't be sure now. The central production on that

occasion could hardly be anything but *Comus*. It is
my favourite memory of Ludlow Castle. The
performance began late in the evening, by
floodlighting, and was staged with the hall range and
the great twelfth-century north-west tower as
backdrop. It had been a hot and sunny summer day,
the cool of the evening was gentle and sweet-
scented, and as the full darkness came the world
outside the floodlights disappeared, and might as
well have disintegrated for all we knew or cared.
The Attendant Spirit delivered the last long,
wonderful speech from the top of the tower, a
single flood on him, and out of the ripe grasses
thousands upon thousands of little silvery moths had
gathered to the light, so that the speaker – and he
was a fine speaker – was surrounded by clouds of
minute angelic witnesses, silver dancing sparks like
the dust of stars.

Westward from Ludlow long uplands of old
forest stretch, the Whitcliffe Wood prolonging its
lofty ridge into Bringewood Chase. The northern
slopes from the crest of the ridge are in Shropshire,
the southern in Herefordshire, and through the easy
valley to the north the Teme winds its way down to
Ludlow and beyond. At one spot on the river, under
the flank of the Chase, the Knights, eighteenth-
century ironmasters, had a forge and a wharf. They
had acquired land in this very beautiful stretch of

country, in the first place for the timber of the forest, but they saw the possibilities of such splendid sites as the dramatic hills and valleys here provided, and built themselves a castle in the true Romantic style. Downton Castle is over the border in Herefordshire, but the forge is barely a quarter of a mile out of Shropshire. From its industrial occupation it resigned long ago; it is now a beautifully organized enhancement of the Knights' estate, designed to provide the dramatic and elegant spectacle obligatory in a truly Romantic landscape, to complete the view from the castle. They built a lovely, single-arch bridge of white stone over the Teme, and beneath it on the upstream side a semi-circular weir in the same polished whiteness. Trees come down to the water on either bank. From the crest of the arch the castle on its sheer hill upstream is just visible, as bridge and weir are just, most satisfyingly, visible from the castle.

I was there once in a February thaw, when the sun was fleetingly out, pale but brilliant, and everywhere there seemed to be the trickling of water, even in the grass, which was bright green from all the rains, and brightly white with snowdrops. The river was full, and the graceful parapets of the bridge are broad but low. Standing on the crest and facing upstream, stunned by the roar of the weir, I could feel the compulsion and turbulence of the air displaced by the rushing water pulling me strongly forward. To lean over would have been to risk flowing down with the Teme. There was always something oblique and sinister in the Romantic landscape. The sense of menace was part of its attraction.

Bridgnorth, though smaller, is the hill town *par excellence*, perched on a lofty red sandstone cliff. Approached from below, and viewed across the level watermeadows and the Severn, it reminds me of the distant view of Langres, in the Haute Marne. The abrupt escarpment unrolls as a high but level skyline, an acropolis, with the main town deployed with confidence along the plateau. Here there is also the ruin of a castle, naturally placed at the commanding western prow of the rock, but from a distance the two vertical accents of the church towers provide the necessary and satisfying focus for the eyes. At the castle end is Telford's classical church of St Mary Magdalen, at the other the red sandstone of St Leonard's. St Mary's is part of the castle site, and replaces the castle chapel. Close to it a garden encloses the ruins of the castle itself, slighted in the Civil War. The formidable keep, tipped out of true by explosives, leans at an angle that puts the Tower of Pisa to shame, but it has preserved its eccentric equilibrium for several centuries now, and shows no sign of giving up.

There has been a fortress of some sort here since before the Normans came. The hill has seen its share of storm, siege and sack, from Henry I early in the twelfth century to the Parliamentarians in the middle of the seventeenth.

St Mary's church provides the closing harmony at the end of one of the most urbane and gracious town streets in England, East Castle Street. On a more modest and domestic scale than Ludlow's Broad Street, but equally Georgian in effect, this short cul-de-sac presents an ideal picture of temperate, civilized residential felicity, a fine place to live. When you discover that all the houses on its happier side have gardens behind running down to overlook a superb view of the river far below, the handsome bridge crossing it, and the gracious fields and wooded sandstone hills beyond, a dwelling here seems even more desirable. The Castle Walk along the hillside, just below these garden boundaries, was considered by Charles II 'the finest walk in my kingdom'.

This is the private face of Bridgnorth. Not secretive, simply decently reserved. The public face is in the broad expanse of the High Street, with the north gate of the town — admittedly much restored — closing it at one end, thus slowing up the traffic to ensure that all eyes appreciate the fine vista about to open before them; and the Town Hall, with its timbered upper storey braced on open ground floor arches, placed sturdily in the middle of the street. Here beats the prosperous heart of a market town drawing upon a whole region as custom for its goods and services, and supplying not only the sophisticated articles and artefacts so wide a range of tastes demands, but also acting as a centre of social and cultural life.

Bridgnorth, like Shrewsbury, finding its hilltop fully occupied, naturally continued to grow where there was still room, down below by the river. There are several ways of getting from Low Town to High Town. At one time the steep and winding Cartway, leading up from the bridge to the end of the High Street, was literally the only cartway available. Now there is a motor road winding round the further end of the rock outcrop to emerge beside the castle. There is a rock-cut staircase, the Stoneway Steps, climbing from Severnside. And there is the shortest and steepest cliff railway in England, said to mount a gradient of two in three. And in contrast to the suave houses at the summit, there are caves in many places in the sandstone cliff-face that were occupied as dwellings, reputedly from Saxon times, and some as late as this century.

In its flatter countryside and more easterly position, Shropshire's Newport shows the same self-confident and composed face, and some of the same essential components, the wide, impressive main street, charters going back to Henry I, an important church founded in the twelfth century, and still boasting its fourteenth-century tower attached to a more modern chancel and nave, and a hinterland of mixed farming and county estates which enlarges the scope of its shopping facilities by demand. The general impression is again Georgian, relaxed, assured and comfortable with its image.

Shifnal, on a slightly smaller scale, follows the same pattern. Much Wenlock keeps an older manner, being the protégé of a great Cluniac priory in its origins, and still owing its undoubted distinction to the remaining splendours of that house. Compact and homogeneous, built almost entirely of local stone, it has neither grown nor declined, but keeps its quality and its moderation with grace and good sense.

The towns of the northern plain are of a somewhat different emphasis, though their history is as long, for every one of them is recorded in Domesday. Ellesmere, Market Drayton, Wem, Whitchurch, all of them set in rich agricultural land, and all natural clearing-houses for the produce of the land, markets for corn, dairy products, agricultural produce and stock, both cattle and sheep. All had early churches, but all are now either totally replaced because of being reduced to ruin, or much restored. Their market charters date from as far back as Henry III, and they all retain recollections of the Middle Ages, but the Georgian influence is generally overriding. In this century their function, in this pleasant rolling country, is to facilitate distribution and communication, and prosper accordingly.

Nevertheless, they all have their individual flavour. Ellesmere presides over its own Lake District, with several large meres and a host of smaller lakelets centred round it and scattered further to eastward, the legacy of the last glaciation, which left its moraine material over all the north of the shire, dropped its boulders many miles from where it had picked them up, spread its alluvial mud over the land, and elbowed rivers into changed courses. The mere country is gentle and beautiful, an attraction to yachtsmen, oarsmen, waterfowl and naturalists, and with a flora including a number of rareties. Further east, round Whixall, it changes into peat mosses and becomes a landscape of placid brown waters, marsh plants and canal drawbridges.

Oswestry, very much an embattled border town, peers eastward into the alluvial plains of middle England, and westward into the rising hills of Wales. Oswald, its patron saint, Christian king of Northumbria, died here at the hands of pagan King Penda of Mercia after defeat at the battle of

Maserfield, one of those all too real and yet semi-legendary seminal battles of the early Christian Church. Much that was old has of necessity been lost here, since the town paid the price of being a frontier fortress, and three times over was destroyed by fire. But the sense of the past remains strong without the need of more reminders than a few stones of the castle, and copies of ancient charters. Like Shrewsbury itself, Oswestry has been in and out of Wales in its time, and as usual on ground once bitterly disputed, is as much Welsh as it is English, and speaks both with equal fluency.

Oswestry means something very special to me since I broke a vertebra in a fall, and spent ten weeks in the Robert Jones and Agnes Hunt Orthopaedic Hospital three miles or so north of the town. This is the pioneer hospital in the world in its own field. As a long-stay patient there you become one of a close if large family, so familial that no one has a surname, and age, sex, status go for nothing. Being all in the same boat welds people into a crew capable of staying afloat and getting their craft into port against all the odds. Misfortune itself is a very mysterious and incalculable thing, sometimes recalled with real affection. I had a great deal of fun in the spinal injuries wards, and found out a great deal about what is and what is not disability.

Oswestry is also the most celebrated home of the

hot-air balloon, and thanks to Per Lindstrand takes pride in the industry and the sport. One of our nurses was the proud part-owner of a balloon, and took part, while I was a patient, in an expedition to Russia to show the flag at an international gathering, and came back to report with justifiable satisfaction that she had flown the local mayor – or whatever is the appropriate title in a Russian town – in her balloon. Even when lying flat on your back you find that your mind can soar.

And there between hospital and town is Old Oswestry: forty acres of Iron Age hill-fort, with its multiple defences of dyke and ditch, abandoned since the Romans came.

Market Drayton presides over the north-eastern corner of the county, on an elevated bank overlooking the upper waters of the River Tern, with heathland east of it in Staffordshire. Its name indicates its function. The market grant goes back to Henry III, and provided a clearing-house for dairy cattle and dairy produce, with easy access eastward into the central shires of England. Whitchurch, at the northerly tip of the shire, looks towards Cheshire and provides the same service of a gateway to the northern counties. The White Church from which it takes its name has been replaced now by a fine eighteenth-century one, with a tall tower that provides a landmark for miles around. Again the accent in the streets is chiefly Georgian, gracious, dignified and durable. But in all these towns, seldom called upon for centuries to act as fortresses, their Norman castles are now green mounds, with perhaps a few stones left by way of reminder. These are business and transport towns, embedded firmly in prosperous agricultural country, their own industries light and genteel; their history is as long as that of the western border towns, but generally less stormy. The Civil War of the seventeenth century split the county almost equally between Cavaliers and Parliamentarians, and slighted a few castles about the shire, and precipitated a few sieges, but once that turmoil was over the towns of Shropshire settled down to a solid, comfortable existence of moderate growth, sturdily retaining their rights, charters and markets, and well aware of the respect due to their craftsmen, tradesmen and civic dignitaries.

Change, if and when it came, was gradual and not too hard to assimilate. The drastic change of the New Town concept was not yet either a threat or a promise.

FOUR

IRON AGE

Not the Iron Age of the hillforts on Brown Clee and Old Oswestry and the Wrekin, and almost every other notable summit along the borders, but of the Reynolds family, and the Darbys, and the Simpsons, all those Quaker families that brought about the revolution in heavy industry, transport and techniques generally, from the exploitation of the canal system to the development of the railways, from the revolutionary use of coke for smelting iron to the refinement of machinery in almost every branch of industry. Everyone knows their names. There is hardly anything new to be said about them. The Industrial Revolution began here, one of those sudden frenetic leaps forward in human self-discovery and expertise that erupt from time to time, with incalculable results for good or ill, or sometimes both together.

I was born in the region of the change. My father and my brother both were employed in Horsehay Ironworks, and my schooldays were overshadowed for the older generation of those parts by the slump of the late twenties and early thirties, when men were laid off in great numbers, and without the cushioning of social protection that exists now. That was the reverse of the golden coin. The high period began in the early eighteenth century, and brought jobs, celebrity and prosperity to the Coalbrookdale coalfield, when the first of the Abraham Darby dynasty succeeded in using coke, instead of the charcoal of the diminishing forests, to smelt iron. The horizon of industry exploded, the new techniques proliferated over the world.

The gorge of the Severn, as is generally held, owes its very existence to the last glaciation, the same which spread its boulder clays and alluvial deposits over all the north of the county. The river, it is believed, originally flowed north, but the blocking of that exit to the sea raised its level and force to the point when it gouged its way through the hilly barrier of Wenlock Edge and poured triumphantly away on its present-day course, sheering through the narrows and shouldering hills and rocks aside, a tremendous force of nature. Behold its meandering course a couple of miles upstream, and then watch thaw-water streaming down past Ironbridge in late February, sweeping miniature icebergs along with it, and you can understand and believe in the change. In the eighteenth century the geological formation with its wealth of coal and iron ore, and the brains and perseverance of man, turned the gorge into an equally formidable force yet again, a red-hot core shooting sparks to the ends of the earth, and gave birth to a dazzling array of firsts: the first iron bridge, the first iron rails, the first iron boat, and a generation of great Quaker ironmasters. All but one. John Wilkinson was no Quaker. Why, in any case were these pioneers so predominantly Quaker? The persuasion certainly believed in education and gave much attention to it, they believed in humanity, they were not afraid of change, they had an optimism and a stability of belief that gave them immense innovative courage. Industrial labour then, even in the best employment, was tough enough, but with the Quaker masters I think it was among the best employment to be had.

But why did all this Christian energy and force go into industry? Was it that in the absence of a permitted sensitivity to the arts it had to go somewhere, and the new flowering of industrial processes made that an acceptable channel? I am told, but can hardly believe, that they did not allow music in their houses, which might be an indication of deprivation. But is it true? I simply do not know. If true, I find it very sad. They deserve transcendent music, religious, human, humane.

At any rate, there they were, almost all the most

prominent, Quakers. They showed excellent ingenuity and imagination in more directions than heavy industry, and more materials than iron. The Reynolds dynasty laced our county and others with a tracery of poised and beautiful waterways by which the products of industry could be distributed. The appeal of the canal to the orderly mind must be its universal respect for level and proportion. By its very nature it must, like the medieval terraced ploughing on sloping land, pay due homage to contour, and thereby necessarily produces a weaving, graceful line wherever it goes. It is an artform, and not the least.

The first of the Reynolds dynasty, Richard, was one of the ironmasters, and a leading member of the linked community of illustrious families which developed all the major industries of the district in a kind of loose but amiable association for mutual enlightened self-interest. The very same practical consideration, in fact, which gave rise to the developments in transport by water, as the cheapest and most expeditious way of bringing the industrial materials together for production. John Randall, the local historian who left copious and anecdotal records of all the goings-on in the coalfield region in the late nineteenth century, describes the achievements of William Reynolds, Richard's elder son:

His name is associated with every important work of improvement in the district during the latter end of the last and the beginning of the present centuries, and especially with a very ingenious contrivance by means of which the inequalities of surface were overcome and the old fashioned locks were dispensed with.

This was the inclined plane, which could convey container-boats up and down a double-tracked slope from one level of water to another many feet lower, the descending load hoisting a rising one with up to a third the same weight aboard. He brought one branch on high ground to a point above Coalbrookdale, and another above Coalport, tackling differences of level of 73 feet in one case and 207 feet in the other. A whole network of minor canals and railed tracks developed, to connect the many furnaces and works in the region. Later, when railway fever took possession of both public and experts, some canal levels, being so adaptable to another use, were cannibalized into the tracks. Later again, when the railways in their turn fell into decline, those same contoured routes reverted to walkways. But in several places I knew in childhood brief sections of level waterway survived, going nowhere, in the corners of fields or bisecting a piece of waste ground, gradually drying out until they grassed over and left curious green ditches. And the planned reservoirs originally made to feed and top up the channels, some planted with old, fine trees along their waterside paths, became wilderness lakes of great beauty, and finally were incorporated, in at least one case, into the park of a new, planned town.

But for several generations everything was iron. The iron bridge that gives Ironbridge its name is the most famous symbol of all, and the most beautiful, with its reflection in the river a perfect circle, and elegant and graceful in its filigree metalwork. That was the joint creation of Abraham Darby III and his contemporaries. But the Coalbrookdale works made many other things of iron: decorative plaques with scenes as elaborate as The Last Supper, huge cauldron cooking pots for Africa, tombstones, gophering irons, doorstops, garden ornaments, besides the massive engineering components chiefly associated with the metal. A tontine of ironmasters built the Tontine Hotel to house their business visitors. Other industries sat cheek by jowl, the Coalport chinaworks, the tileworks of Jackfield, the clay pipes, including the celebrated 'churchwardens' of Broseley, Broseley brick and tile . . . the list is long and the cross-fertilization total. Scions of other illustrious families mingle and intermarry with the Darbys and Reynoldses – Rathbones, Cranages, Anstices, Randalls, Roses. Some of them were polymaths of almost Renaissance breadth, chemists, geologists, engineers, surveyors, writers and historians. In their heyday they made this Shropshire coalfield and its environs so celebrated that poets of the Romantic school wrote awed panegyrics on its fearful, burning splendour, and painters like Loutherbourg repeatedly displayed its furnaces and fires on canvas.

The decline came when the wars which had kept the fires fed for so long came to an uneasy respite, demand for iron fell, and one by one the furnaces were blown out, and later one by one the pits closed.

It must have been about 1947 or 1948, I think, when I joined a Sunday morning conducted party to visit the Kemberton pit, and in borrowed boiler suit and miner's helmet crawled on hands and knees along the low coalface, and rode down a sloping passage afterwards on the tubs. That was one of the last local pits to go, but it has been closed now for many years. The industrial landscape, long in decline, and overgrown into a wild kind of beauty and richness in many places, is now taking a fresh turn in its long and varied history, for our iron age has become history in the most serious way, the object of intense study and passionate interest.

The early furnace of the Darby family, the Coalbrookdale works, the Coalport chinaworks, the

Bedlam furnaces, Ironbridge itself, the wharf on the Severn, all are incorporated now into the Ironbridge Gorge Museum, which has grown up gradually over the past twenty years or so into a major tourist attraction, but also, I hope, a serious record of an age of achievement which changed the world, for good or ill. The inclined planes have been cleared out and restored, the kilns of Coalport show their proudest display wares again, the historic furnace is preserved under cover, the old arts are demonstrated, live, tiles are made again at Jackfield. The world to which the sparks of the Darby furnaces flew to kindle fresh fires comes back to the place where it all began, to see and marvel.

The main part of this living museum is the open-air range of Blist's Hill — Randall's history calls it 'Blisser's Hill', but local versions do vary. This is the whole of the wild, wooded slope that descends steeply from Madeley to the Severn at Coalport, and includes the inclined plane, a section of the canal above, and the industrial remains of the pits and furnaces left behind by the Reynolds and Anstice families. All manner of other items appropriate to the time and the subject have been transferred to the site from other places — Victorian chapel, pub, pharmacy, sweetshop, a printshop, a candle shop, Telford's tollhouse from the A5, and a section of his road-surfacing.

Years ago, when the museum was only a vague idea for the future, my brother and I spent an autumn afternoon among the broken levels and industrial ruins of Blist's Hill taking photographs. The whole site was deserted and overgrown, but the engine-house remains and the brambles and bushes and outcrops of cinder presented a romantic image in autumnal earth-tones of russet and gold and brick red, and all the variations of green fading into brown. The effect was strangely like a series of eighteenth-century paintings of aristocratic, contrived landscapes, with the gaunt engine-houses for ruined castles. Now the place is peopled again, lively with visitors in the summer, staging weekends Victorian style, events involving horses in harness, seasonal celebrations of all kinds. I still remember it as it was, with a kind of melancholy pleasure.

Among the small domestic items made in cast iron at Coalbrookdale were many little figures, some meant as garden decorations, some as doorstops. In John Randall's *History of Madeley*, he discusses the wide powers of the borough justices, and the abuses sometimes practised by unscrupulous constables, who were allowed to carry blank warrants and occasionally used them against vagrants or strangers at random, for no offence at all. He quotes the case of three itinerant Dutch girls thus victimized, and adds, 'Buy-a-

Brooms, as they were called'. We had from as far back as I can remember, and I still have, a cast-iron doorstop which was always referred to as the Buy-a-Broom, so evidently such Dutch girls travelling locally here and selling twig brooms were a well-known phenomenon, though I have never seen them mentioned elsewhere. The lady is about 9 inches tall, dressed in a laced bodice and a full, short skirt, with a 'kerchief on her head, and carrying brooms on her back. One of them looms over her shoulder, a second originally jutted above her head, but that one is broken off. Cast iron is hard but brittle. She must be a Coalbrookdale piece, almost everything for miles around in iron stems from the same works.

The iron fever is gone, the railway fever is gone, many of the works are closed. Enthusiasts re-opened a stretch of the Severn Valley railway years ago, and have extended it since to link with the national network again, a triumph of love. Immaculately maintained locomotives keep steam alive on a beautiful line, and the proud members lavish loving care on their rolling stock and stations. What remains of the great ironmasters is the wealth of fine Georgian houses with which they adorned the streets of Broseley and the dramatic hillside terraces of Ironbridge and Coalbrookdale.

I went to school in Coalbrookdale from the age of eleven, and the High School – girls one end, boys the other, and shared rooms such as hall, art room and laboratory amidships — lay at the very end of the Dale as it emerges into the river valley. In flood seasons the Coal Brook often backed up from the Severn and covered the school gates, or at least ours, which lay slightly lower than the boys'. I remember at least one winter thaw when substantial ice-floes were coming clashing down the narrows of the river. Memory enhances everything, I know, but in the Severn gorge weather and season were always exciting. I walked down the steep and unstable hill known as the Jiggers Bank, with lavishly treed cliffs on one hand and the deep wooded cleft of the brook on the other. There were caves in the cliff at one point, and the ruined remains of a bridge over the brook below. Nothing in that region could ever resist a touch of drama.

The 'jigger' was the man who controlled by a brake the speed of the cars on the steep industrial tramways laid on the slopes round the Dale, one of which ran up the Jiggers Bank, my way down to school later, when the rails were all long gone. The gradient was considerable. Often on early winter mornings I would set out from Horsehay at the top in brilliant unclouded light, and half-way down the hill would wade into a level sea of thick mist drowning the valley below. At other times this order was reversed, I set out in mist, and half-way down the hill emerged into sunshine and a cloudless sky, the change being astonishingly abrupt and clearcut.

The deep valley of the brook, wooded and rich in wild flowers and bird-life, was known as the Lum Hole. I have no idea exactly how it got the name, but it was one of our favourite playgrounds as children. Who could resist a wilderness threaded by a lively brook, full of primroses and bluebells and celandine and anemones every spring, and rendered slightly sinister by its broken bridge, no light timber skeleton but with solid masonry and brick abutments. I think there must have been a very early forge there, making use of the water for power and the abundant trees for charcoal, long before Abraham Darby experimented with coke, and changed the world.

FIVE

Of Castles, Mansions and Ruins

Like the greater part of humanity, we Salopians are a hybrid lot. Since all racial migrations, apparently, came in drives from the east, the dwellers on the western fringes always received and incorporated into their own bloodstock those remnants pressed on to the defensive by the succeeding invasion. It would seem that neither men of the Stone Ages nor the Bronze Age have left much trace in our county, perhaps because, even after the last glaciation period ended, soil and climate and vegetation rendered it too inhospitable, and only when the iron tools improved, and provided ploughs that could tackle heavy glacial clays, and axes capable of hacking out an assart from dense oak forest, did men settle here in any great numbers. A few long barrows do indicate that even earlier the land was not totally deserted. Those who died here must first have lived here. But the more frequent round burial mounds and the great hill-forts came in with the Britons, the tall, fair people of the second Celtic wave, who settled here in considerable numbers, installed themselves with determination, and fought it out with the Romans when those relentlessly organized legionaries arrived in the land.

Here in the west the tall, fair people withdrew into the uplands on the heels of the small, wiry, dark people they had driven there before them. And when there was nowhere further west to go except into the sea, they all in their turn, or their remnants, stayed and made the best of it, and tolerated and intermarried and traded with those they had driven into the hills in their own aggressive heyday.

It happened even to the Romans themselves in the end. They had founded as their advance headquarters towards Wales the town of Uriconium, our earliest major site of archaeological and even architectural interest in Shropshire. At first it was simply a military base in hostile territory, but later, when the country round it had grown used to the invaders, and the Cornovii were pacified into acceptance, Uriconium was enlarged and adorned as a classical Roman city, with noble public buildings, forum, baths and shops, where Britons and Romans lived, traded and socialized side by side. It is impressive enough as it appears now, but for many acres around, the folded and sculptured outlines of the fields suggest that what we see is only a fraction of what is hidden from us. Time-expired legionaries, for years familiar with this land, took their bounty and settled here, married native wives, stayed when the legions at last retreated to save Rome itself, and left Uriconium to decline gradually until the next wave of Saxons caused it to be abandoned, and the remaining population withdrew to what is now Shrewsbury, a defensible site in its coil of river.

No doubt every intermarriage among all these tribal rivals, enemies and finally allies, has contributed to the character of the border Englishman through the centuries, and the border Welshman too. And each succeeding generation changed the nature of the county to some extent, in its manner of farming, building, living. The Romans, based on Uriconium, provided a network of roads which still serve today. They left their traces in the long, relentlessly straight stretches of road to be found heading for Montgomery, near Acton Burnell, and in several other places, and at Ruckley, under Lodge Hill, where there is a section of the original surface still left, laid with great stones, and it crosses the Chatwall Brook by a small Roman bridge built of the same stones. Naturally the local name for it is the Devil's Causeway. The devil is always the intruder, the stranger, the one who is different. Every successive wave of newcomers from the mainland of Europe, either from the north or the east, was the very devil in its day.

All these early ancestors of ours were too remote in time to leave us the most intimate evidence of what they were like, their dwellings and the furnishings within them, the possessions they valued, the amenities they enjoyed. But later ages leave us a wealth of such evidence, and there is nothing human curiosity loves more than a glimpse of how the other half lives. Peering into other men's homes, stately or modest, is endlessly enlightening and intriguing.

The Normans, the latest devils to manifest their presence among us by simple invasion, were great builders, and if their first castles were thrown up in a hurry in timber to cope with immediate native resentment, as soon as they felt established they went to work with durable materials like stone, and barring siege and slighting, their works stayed up. Of castles, Shropshire has plenty, from huge and formidable piles like Ludlow to the green mounds of grass and trees that are all that remain of Caus and Holdgate, and many others along the border. The outer line standing guard on the very edge of

Wales is strung out from north to south, from Oswestry and Whittington through Alberbury, Caus and Bishop's Castle to Clun and Hopton in the south. Some of these are merely mottes now. Whittington and Clun still present imposing if fragmentary ruins. The supporting strong points east of these border fortresses have almost all been smoothed away into the landscape, though the traces of their foundations persist. Deeper into the interior of the county castles like those at Wem, Bridgnorth, Holdgate, Shrewsbury, Cleobury Mortimer and Ludlow were centres of administration, caputs of baronies, the chief seats of scattered and powerful honours.

The wonderful thing about real ruins, sculpted by wear and tear and time, is that those fragments which are left standing almost always seem to compose themselves into the most noble and attractive shapes, as if they had selectively discarded what was not necessary to the appropriate effect; while those artificial ruins placed on high spots in their estates by ambitious eighteenth-century landowners, with every advantage of being specially designed to emulate that same effect, very frequently miss the target, and look just what they are, false and totally without function. There is a strong impulse to beauty in the functional. These early stone castles were built to serve a very urgent and specific function, and even in ruin they sustain the dignity and justification of their purpose.

Even the stark green mottes to be found tucked away behind barns or in churchyards, abrupt, surprisingly small, and often thickly covered with bushes and trees round their sloping sides, where windblown or bird-carried seeds first lodge, heave up their bushy shoulders sturdily, self-assured in their reminder of former power and menace.

This propensity for trapping seeds, and clothing their flanks with new trees is something castle mottes share with the deserted monuments of power in later ages, the pennystone pit mounds of the early nineteenth century, after a hundred years grown into groves of established woodland and haunts of bird-song. A natural process of repair and restitution finds ways of bestowing unexpected grace upon all evidences of the outworn and discarded preoccupations of man.

But the Normans built other things besides castles. The most beautiful and haunting of all ruins are the remains of those monastic houses founded and endowed by kings, bishops, barons and earls for the well-being of their own souls, perhaps, above all else, but also to the great gain of succeeding generations, for whom their foundations provided the chief source of education, charity and medicine, the principle encouragement of libraries and scholarship, and the most reliable patronage for skills in music and the arts.

Of Shropshire's major monastic foundations only the two Benedictine houses of Shrewsbury and Bromfield have managed to preserve their churches for parish use, if somewhat mangled after the Dissolution. At Bromfield events took a very odd turn when the property passed into the hands of one Charles Foxe, who blocked up the chancel arch and incorporated the chancel in a new Tudor house for himself. But in 1658 it reverted to church property after the Tudor building burned down. Of the priory nothing remains but a fine, large gatehouse, built of stone below, and timber-framed above. Bromfield was an independent priory for only about fifty years, and then the brothers, in 1155, opted to present themselves and the priory's possessions in lands to the abbey of St Peter at Gloucester, and remained as a cell of that house until the Dissolution.

There were two great houses of Augustinian canons in the county, both in beautiful settings, and both still preserving impressive remains. Haughmond is slightly the older of the two, founded by William FitzAlan in 1135, though most of what remains is from later in the twelfth century, and further additions and elaborations in the succeeding centuries. As in so many cases, part of the fabric was transformed into a Tudor mansion after the Dissolution, but the Tudor house is gone, while quite substantial parts of the abbey itself are still standing. The site slopes, and the walls at the east end back firmly into the rock of Haughmond Hill, richly treed. There is a splendid entrance to the chapter house, three arches, the flanking pair slightly lower and narrower than the central one, which houses the actual doorway, while the other two hold smaller windows. Elegant shafts with foliage capitals separate the arches. The range of the infirmary and the abbot's lodging are later, but just as notable. There is something particularly gracious about the colouring of mellowed stone against the bright green of well-kept turf and dark green of trees. In a sequestered setting, drawn aside from a road which is in any case fairly quiet, Haughmond has a serenity and tranquility all its own. The Augustinians seem to have borne a very good reputation in Shropshire, and attracted loyal patrons, for Haughmond was a wealthy and highly respected house.

Its brother-house at Lilleshall presents itself almost as an identical twin, situated in an equally green and pleasant and retired spot, and perhaps with even more of its impressive splendours left to give delight. It was founded a little later than Haughmond, in 1148. It is neighbour now to the nineteenth-century Lilleshall

Hall, built for the Duke of Sutherland, who owned extensive property hereabouts, and incidentally built some of the very best cottage housing for his workmen. On Lilleshall Hill, a rocky outcrop beside the village, there is an obelisk erected to commemorate him. Round about that time there was a fashion for obelisks. The hall has been through several metamorphoses since it was a ducal residence, and is now the National Sports Centre, providing training and encouragement to young sportsmen and women in many fields.

But once within the enclave of the abbey, the wanderer is back in the twelfth and thirteenth centuries, and the outer world vanishes.

Approach from the west, and you are confronted with a massive central doorway, its arch deeply moulded and roundly and unmistakably Norman, though some of the carving of its capitals and hood-mould move on into the field of the particularly English, and particularly beautiful, stiff-leaf, vigorous aspiring foliage, vital enough to hold up vaulted roofs. It is the period and the style I wanted to use as the peak of a great art, and in this manifestation hardly found out of England, in *The Heaven Tree*. That book was conceived not necessarily as an historical novel, but as an attempt to create a credible artist, even a great artist, and to set him in his own society, whatever the period; and whatever the period, I was certain he would find himself to some extent in collision with society, by virtue of the very qualities of proportion and balance that made him an artist. For someone else it could have been set in another period, even this one. For me it began in 1200 or so simply because I regarded the building of the great cathedrals as about the highest achievement of human talent and skill, a peak in art, and the particular excitement of the stiff-leaf carving, its sheer organic energy, truth and power, seemed to me a peak upon a peak. So the time was laid down for me.

Enter this monumental archway at Lilleshall, and the whole great length of the church – Pevsner records it as being 228 feet long – opens before you, and carries the eye onward and out through the great east window, empty of all but the broken edges of its tracery, into the trees and the sky beyond; a wide, round-arched doorway into the church, and a pointed window-arch, tall, almost an oval because of the hollowing of the floor beneath it, letting the imagination out again into a green world.

There are quite substantial remains of the conventual building, too, enough to suggest the status of the house at its height. It enjoyed the profit from tolls on traffic crossing Atcham Bridge over the Severn, but lost them in the fourteenth century, and its income declined accordingly.

We had also, in the county, a small house of Augustinian nuns at White Ladies, very near the Staffordshire border, and the shell of their church remains. The house normally supported only about six ladies, and they did not use the term canoness here, but called themselves nuns.

The one great Cistercian abbey in Shropshire started life not as Cistercian but as Savignac. It was founded by Roger de Clinton, Bishop of Lichfield and Coventry, for grey monks of the order of Savigny. There were thirteen houses of the order in England and Wales, several founded in the same year as our Buildwas, 1135. Some years later the Cistercians had arrived in numbers, and were acquiring influence and power, and the French Savignac houses, and especially the abbot and convent of Savigny itself, were drawn strongly towards the new order, and began to promulgate the notion of joining it *en masse*, with all their daughter-houses. The controversy went on for some time, with the English foundations putting up a strong resistance, but in 1147 at the Cistercian general chapter, with the Pope present, the order of Savigny submitted to Citeaux, and was swallowed up. As would be expected of stubborn Englishmen, the grey monks here took no notice, but went on for another year considering themselves independent, and behaving accordingly. In the next

year Pope Eugenius formally promulgated the order
of union. Furness Abbey, head of the English houses,
still stood out, and the abbot, Peter, set off to make
his appeal to Pope Eugenius in person, with the
inevitable result. Citeaux won. Peter was ordered to
submit, did so, and resigned his office.

To make sure, the abbot of Savigny circularized
all the English houses, ordering them to put off the
grey habit and don the white, and transfer their
allegiance to the Cistercian constitution. Thus
Buildwas became a Cistercian monastery. What the
Shropshire brothers thought about all this is not
recorded.

Dr Nikolaus Pevsner, in the *Shropshire* volume of
the Penguin 'Buildings of England' series, considers
on the evidence of the details that none of the
buildings now remaining can have been begun as
early as 1135, when the foundation is dated, though
from 1147 on, when the change to Citeaux was
accomplished, they may have been in hand. The
general solidity, simplicity and strength of the whole
is thoroughly Norman, but the detail inclines to the
later Norman. The railway which Pevsner deplored
as a detraction from the felicity of the site is gone,
like so many other country lines. It was a section of
the Severn Valley line, beautiful enough in its heyday
to deserve preservation in its own right.

The consistent loveliness of monastic sites, even

before the Cistercians consciously looked for the heads of remote and unfrequented river valleys, makes me wonder if every cloistered soul had a special instinct for beauty, an attraction to paradise here in this world, a stage on the way to the ultimate perfection somewhere beyond. It can hardly have been merely by chance, in the quest for nothing more than withdrawal from the world's distractions. They could have found even remoter and loftier and more solitary places of barren ugliness if that had been all. I cannot believe any race of men ever existed without some instinctive response to the graces of the natural world. The vernacular poetry of the Middle Ages is full of the joy of birds, flowers, the bursting buds of spring, youth, and the company of pleasant women. At any rate, those who chose the sites to build their monasteries hardly ever failed to compose scenes of quite spectacular beauty. And Buildwas is no exception.

It stands on a gracious green level beside the Severn, with wide meadows upstream, through which the river meanders in serpentine curves, and the beginning of the gorge downstream, where the water gathers at speed into the narrows. Weathered grey stone and vivid green of turf again, trees all along the waterside, and steep woodland on either flank where the gorge closes in.

Aligned along this green lawn between rising hills, with the river flowing along its north side, beyond the cloister which here, unusually, lies north of the church, the entire shell of the building deploys to view the seven bays of the nave, powerful round arches upon thick circular piers, the crossing tower, or at least the lower courses of it, broad and formidable as a castle keep, and the square sanctuary of the east end, with its three long, round-arched lancet windows. Very austere, very strong, and extremely handsome. Noble is the word that comes to mind. The year that Buildwas became Cistercian, its founder and original builder joined the second crusade, and the following year he died at the siege of Antioch. He was also the builder of the first Norman church at Lichfield, his cathedral, and I am assured that his building there must strongly have resembled Buildwas. So perhaps the plan, if not the actual fulfilment of it, was his.

Screened from the cloistral buildings by trees, and closed off into a separate garden, the remains of the abbot's lodging were built into a later private residence, which is now a club. North of the church the cloister goes down to the trees and the river, rimmed on the east by the range of transept, crypt, and chapter house, vaulted in nine bays, and approached down a broad stairway. Patterns of masonry in the grass mark where the aisle walls stood, and show the layout of the whole; but one of the chief glories of Buildwas is the massive seven-bay stretch of its open arches, and the framed glimpses of tranquil lawn and trees through every arch. Another, less apparent treasure was its library, from which a number of books have survived in Trinity College, Cambridge, Lambeth Palace, and I believe at least one in Shrewsbury.

Buildwas was the nearest to my childhood home of all the monastic sites, well within what we then considered walking distance, and it was the one I knew best, even before it found its way into the care of what was then the Office of Works, and was cleared up and laid with the turf that shows up stonemasonry so beautifully. A somewhat longer walk, but still acceptable to our family, was to Much Wenlock. This palimpsest of a convent has had three identities and three founders, as if the site, once consecrated, could never be made to surrender to change, but at every destruction would rise phoenix-like from the ashes. In one case probably quite literally ashes, when the Danes attacked and destroyed it.

The first founder was King Merewald of Mercia, in the late seventh century, who planned it as a nunnery for his daughter, the first abbess, who became St Milburga. This was a small church with an apse, of which some traces have been found in excavations, but it lasted only about a hundred and eighty years before the Danes wiped it out. Not long before the Norman invasion it was refounded by Earl Leofric of Mercia, perhaps as a house of secular canons, and about 1080 Earl Roger de Montgomery made the house into an alien priory, bringing over monks from the Cluniac house of La Charité, in the Loire. Much later the link with Cluny was severed and the house became denizen. But everything about the elegance and elaboration of its remains calls to mind the Cluniac predilection for ceremony and ornament, in building, in music, in the liturgy.

Wenlock is different from the Augustinian abbeys in being the support and *raison d'etre* of a town; and a very delightful little town it is. The range of its domestic architecture runs from medieval half-timbered and timber-framed to modest but elegant Georgian, and most of it in local stone and local timber, and probably local brick, too, for Broseley is close. The Guildhall, open below as a market, braced on great oak timbers, sits shoulder to shoulder with the sturdy stone tower of the church, and presents a street scene any town would be proud of. The black and white upper storey, three-gabled, houses the magistrates' courts and the council chamber, oak-panelled, and with a magnificent array of carved chairs and furnishings.

The church is no less distinguished, and a passageway beside the Guildhall leads through to the churchyard, a quiet green space with a rear wall over which it is possible to peer into the abbey's grounds, and a back view of the houses on the street, which is as debonair as the front view.

At the corner by the church the Bull Ring begins at a small corner newsagents, where, as one journalist writing about the town said, 'You feel you should really be asking for *The Anglo-Saxon Chronicle*'. Beyond a stretch of cobbles the lane passes a square stone tower, part of the monastic enclave, and reaches a secluded level under old trees, alongside a stone wall. Everything beyond the wall is hidden by a thick belt of trees and shrubs, and the entrance to the enclosure is a small gate and a flight of steps, and a kiosk at the top. But when you climb the steps and penetrate through the shielding wall of trees you emerge into wonders. Shorn turf and grey stone compose themselves here into a very intricate picture, hard for the layman to decipher. You enter the nave of the church towards the west end, and the bases of the piers mark out the ground for you. Stand where the central west entrance was, and look down the prodigious length of nave, crossing, chancel and Lady chapel to the east end, 350 feet in all. There were eight bays to the nave, seven to the chancel, both aisled, but what

is left, apart from the regular pattern of the pier
bases islanded in the grass, survives in three
separate fragments. But they are giant fragments,
and fragments of a giant. The most substantial is the
mass of the south transept, leading on to the
roofless but important chapter-house and the
infirmary, but the west wall of the north transept is
also standing, part of the west front, and the three
western bays of the south aisle of the nave. The free-
standing fragments are so lofty and so airily poised
that they appear almost like independent pieces of
inspired sculpture in a green outdoor gallery.

The south transept provides the north wall of the
chapter-house. The entrance into the chapter-house
from the cloister is by three fine Norman arches,
and within, its longer walls, the north and south,
are carved in triple tiers of interlaced blind
arcading. Next to the chapter house is the infirmary,
and beyond and at right angles the prior's lodging.
These two buildings, the infirmary with its chapel,
and the superior's lodging, have been turned into an
L-shaped private house which must be one of the
most beautiful in Britain. Up to recent years,
though it was not opened to the public, they could
at least get a glimpse of it from the priory grounds,
from the corner of the frater and the cloister, but it
is now completely closed off. The entire west front
is a glazed gallery on both ground and upper floors,

a grid of two-light windows separated by buttressed stone mullions. The varied colours of the masonry, the fluting of buttresses, mullions and windows all receive and play with the light at every hour of the day. Seven bays between the main buttresses, and each bay bisected again vertically, and yet again, by the slender shafts between the lights; a slanting sun can finger the long frontage with elusive shadows as though plucking the strings of a harp. And above, there is a great, steep expanse of stone-slated roof, subtly tinted. This was the last addition to the buildings of the priory in the fifteenth century. I do know one or two other houses of comparably acceptable size which I find equally beautiful – not all of them in this country, let alone in this county, though one of them is not so many miles away from Wenlock – but I know of none more beautiful.

Of tastes in housing, as in other matters of taste, no point in disputing. But some houses are simply too big to be lived in. Even in civilized Georgian houses, free at least of the draughts and chills of the twelfth-century stone castles, the food must have been cold by the time it had travelled miles of corridor from the kitchens to the dining-room, and with all the comforts the eighteenth century could provide, a handful of human beings in a pile even a third the size of Blenheim or Castle Howard must have felt like exiles from the real world;

infinitesimal creatures able to use only a very few rooms in a huge and empty mausoleum. True, the really monumental palaces like Blenheim were meant to awe the world outside, assert the magnificence of the owner, and turn his rivals green with envy, rather than to ensure his domestic comfort. But I should have expected every household thus exalted to keep the palace for those precise purposes and occasions, and build themselves a nice little warm, manageable manor-house somewhere in the grounds to do their real living in. The Petit Trianon makes sense. Maybe Marie Antoinette wasn't just playing at shepherdesses, after all, but trying to keep her sanity.

We have nothing in Shropshire of the size of Blenheim or Castle Howard, but even some of the Georgian houses here, nine bays wide and two-and-a-half storeys high, seem to me too big to be comfortable. Being born into an age without resident domestic servants, of course, probably makes all the difference to one's outlook. People look at a house, even one they find attractive, and ask themselves: Can I really run this one satisfactorily? And if the answer is in doubt, they look elsewhere.

Times have changed, of course. Time was when the magnates of England had, and needed, enormous households, when their castles had to accommodate a garrison for protection, and an army of retainers, and storage space enough to provide for all this host in the event of a siege. When times became more settled and secure, under strong government, windows grew larger, fortifications were gradually phased out, and crenellations became merely decorative. In Shropshire, round about 1270 to 1280, two very different men set out to build themselves new and impressive houses, each in his degree. We call them both castles, though neither of them is precisely that.

Robert Burnell, Bishop of Bath and Wells and chancellor to Edward I, had already done some ambitious building on to the hall and chapel of his episcopal palace at Wells. He was an extremely powerful and able official, who had the king's complete confidence, and had entertained him at the bishop's ancestral home of Acton Burnell during the parliament held at Shrewsbury to impeach and destroy Prince David of Gwynedd. Bishops had no vote in cases of blood, and Edward had every intention of making this a very bloody case indeed, but probably preferred to withdraw his actual presence while his orders were carried out and the vote for death taken. Hence the stay at Acton Burnell. In the grounds of the present castle there remain the two great gable ends of what was popularly supposed to be the barn where the parliament was held, but Owen and Blakeway

consider that in fact the parliament was held in
Shrewsbury Abbey, and king and bishop
diplomatically withdrew to the latter's home. The
so-called barn, whether barn or hall, must have
belonged to the older house from which the family
sprang.

That was in 1283. The following year the bishop
received licence to crenellate, and permission to
take timber from the royal forests for the building
of his new and imposing home.

The house he built certainly looks like a castle, a
huge, tall red sandstone square, a tower itself, with
an angle tower taller at each corner, some of its
windows lancets, but others broad and by no means
defensive. It has no moat or fortifications, has
plenteous ways in, and all on the ground floor. The
crenellations are a flourish, befitting the grandeur of
the palace, for a palace it is, and the status of its
builder and owner. Moreover, it is set in a low and
secluded position, commanding no special route or
vulnerable approach. And what is particularly
noticeable is that the broad, grassy level on which it
stands is brilliantly green and lush even in dry
seasons. The bishop's chosen site is just short of
being a marsh. Safely short of it, clearly, since the
house still stands solidly in spite of being open and
roofless now, and ruinous in parts. It reminds me of
the great hollow of St David's, where cathedral,

palace, college and all, an enormous weight of masonry, sustains itself defiantly on ground which has the same emerald lushness, and in this case has caused some subsidence which shows in the outward bulge of the cathedral walls and the tilt of the flooring.

There is a nineteenth-century Acton Burnell Hall in the same extensive grounds, but from within the green enclosure you see nothing but the castle itself and its broad, gracious plain of grass, a number of old, fine trees striking dramatic attitudes close to the walls, and round the whole silent scene more trees, a green shell keep surrounding and framing the bishop's achievement. He built the church, too, a very fine church and close to its patron's walls, but even that is screened from view. A small gate and a narrow footpath through thick dark shrubberies lets you into the secret place, or did so when last I was there, which is some years ago. To be there alone is the ideal, with no occasion for anything louder than a bird to break the silence.

At the other house built at much the same time, perhaps begun ten years earlier, the atmosphere is quite different. Stokesay, one of the gems not just of Shropshire but of England, is a social house, a gregarious house, where there should be voices, conversation, laughter and movement, and ideally, music. Here it is no offence, but beautifully right, to

see children running about the lawns in the
courtyard, and girls waving to their friends below
from the top of the tower, and family parties
carrying trays of tea and cakes from the gatehouse
to seats tucked into the corners of the perimeter
wall.

The man who built this one was a wool
merchant, Laurence of Ludlow. He did not get his
licence to crenellate until 1291, when he was
planning the addition of the tower that justifies the
name castle. Laurence began with a single earlier
stone tower on the site, and built out from it a long
and noble hall range, four-gabled on the courtyard
face, four-gabled to the outer world, and he felt
secure enough to fill in all those gables with tall
windows of two lights. So secure could an
Englishman feel around 1280, even so close to the
borders of Wales! Nor did he surround his property
except with a very modest wall, though he did give
himself a fine deep moat. Under the north tower is
a basement with the well in it, and from the hall a
broad wooden staircase leads up to two chambers in
the top of the tower. At the other end of the hall is
the solar range, which came probably with the south
tower, about 1295, after Laurence got his licence.
But the family's retiring-room as we see it now is
comfortably lined with Elizabethan panelling, has a
splendid fireplace, and two peepholes in the

panelling, to keep an eye on any untoward goings-on in the hall below.

The older north tower is no taller than the roof of the hall that adjoins it, and at some later time someone capped the squat stone portion with a timbered fantasy containing the upstairs rooms, the black and white level projecting from the stone and supported by timber struts, with steeply-pitched tiled roof above, like a peaked hat worn low over the brows. There is nothing quite like it anywhere else. The added south tower by contrast is what one expects of a tower, strong, slit-windowed, dominating the house, and crowned by 7 foot battlements and a small turret over the courtyard corner. Its shape is faceted in a complex way, but achieves an appearance of total and assured harmony. From any angle you can discover, Stokesay is photogenic. And the house itself is but the beginning of its felicities.

There is the gatehouse, by which the visitor enters the walled enclosure and crosses the moat. The lower floor that frames the great studded door is of stone, but the storey above it is of the very gayest Elizabethan black-and-white, gable-ended and with a gable over the doorway, with a wealth of carving on its black framing timbers, a fairy-tale building. And the moat beneath is dry, and has been for years a garden instead of a moat, planted with fruit trees, shrubs and flowers. Even the grass around the trees and bushes down there is mown into smooth lawn. Within the containing wall, which is no more than breast-high, there is a slope of grass rising slightly to the hall doorway, and rimmed with more flowerbeds. On a good day in summer, with small children tumbling about on the grass in bright colours, and running in and out of the huge dim doorway of the hall, everything seems to be bursting into bloom, and there can be no doubt in any mind that Stokesay is a happy place.

It has everything. It is fantastic enough to be astonishing, small enough to be intimate and friendly, and sheerly lovely enough to be remembered for ever, once seen.

I remember once, some years ago, standing at the head of the broad staircase in the great hall, close beneath the lowest reaches of the timbered roof. All the crevices among the slats and beams of the great cave of roof were full of swallows' nests, most of them with young broods aboard, and the parent birds were flashing in and out constantly on the endless labour of feeding them, and the whole air was filled with their excited conversation. They are not only gregarious birds, but voluble, their voices shrill and gay. I hope they still come. I feel sure they do. Why should they desert so desirable and commodious a residence? I feel, too, that swallows have an instinctive sense of whether a chosen place is wretched or blessed.

The list of fine houses in Shropshire is a long one, and I can claim acquaintance with only a few of them. It would take an expert to detail and compare the felicities of all. But to some, once seen, you return again and again, and season by season, and in many weathers, discover them afresh at every visit. Stokesay is the most compulsive of all. Its welcome is personal, like visiting friends, which is remarkable in a dwelling of such early date, and its sturdy domesticity and middle-class provenance are an encouragement to honest ambition in us ordinary mortals. Laurence of Ludlow was a self-made man, and a living witness to the fact of social mobility even in feudal times. Few of his baronial overlords can have had half so lovely a dwelling-place.

Brick came rather late into Shropshire's major building plans. Not until the late years of Henry VIII, about 1540 and on, a century after Ralph, Lord Cromwell, Henry VI's treasurer, put up the tower house to end tower houses at Tattershall in Lincolnshire, in locally-made bricks produced under the tutelage of Dutch and German overseers, brick being more familiar in those countries. Two brick houses were being built here about the same time, though one of them had a second phase of building forty years later. Plaish and Upton Cressett are both in brick, Plaish with stone dressings, both with some decoration in blue brick diapering. They began about the same time, but Upton Cressett had another burst of energetic building later, and to this later period Professor Pevsner attributes the feature which is best known, and in fact shoulders the hall itself into insignificance. Upton Cressett gatehouse is large and dominant, gabled, with tall chimney-stacks at the two outward corners, and pointed turrets at the corners towards the house. It has two full storeys above the ground floor, where the entrance archway leads through to the house beyond.

Though only a mile or so from the main Wenlock-Bridgnorth road, Upton Cressett, in its own way, is the end of the world, for only one narrow road makes its way to the place, and the road goes no further. There is nothing there but the house and gatehouse, and the church, solitary on their hill. Plaish Hall, on the other hand, seems to be at the centre of everything in its particular tract of country, and yet extremely elusive. So, at least, my brother and I found it on one occasion when we were spending a Sunday afternoon driving at random among the narrow network of roads that makes a labyrinth of the triangle loosely between Shrewsbury, Stretton and Much Wenlock. The most rural parts of Shropshire are a web of perilous little roads, all of which lead to the most entrancing places, but none of which provides room for more than one modest car, or any crossing-places, so that if two vehicles meet nose to nose one of them must back, probably a considerable way. Wear and tear on the nerves leads to avoidance of these otherwise desirable routes, especially as the natives there know them every inch, and assume they are the only ones who ever use them, and everyone else should know it.

In our meanderings we began to notice at every junction of these deceptive lanes a signpost saying firmly 'Plaish 1'. It appeared that Plaish was precisely one mile from everywhere in this piece of country. Never having been there, we turned into one of the designated roads. Have you ever noticed how, if you set out on a definite quest, at the next meeting or parting of ways there are three to choose from, and either no signpost at all, or one that fails to mention the place you are seeking? It is a game rural districts play, but I have no quarrel with it; you almost always find somewhere just as pleasant, possibly even more interesting. But after being beguiled two or three times by 'Plaish 1' we did find it at last, and at least four roads really do meet there.

The house was built by Sir William Leighton, Chief Justice of Wales, about 1540, in red brick with stone dressings and some use of blue brick. It is H-shaped, a central hall block and wings that project both fore and aft, with windows stone-mullioned and transomed, very handsome and mellow, and worth finding. Sir William is in Cardington church now, in an elaborate monument, robed, lying on his side and resting his head on his hand, and with all his mourning family deployed about him.

After this period begins the great exuberant, optimistic and self-confident age of Elizabeth, when everyone who could build seemed to be building, when foreign ventures had enlivened every art with new ideas, and merchant prosperity had enabled the burgesses of towns like Shrewsbury to raise splendid memorials to their own success and their ambitions for their children. Shropshire has Elizabethan houses by the score, and in a dazzling variety of styles. In the towns the wealthy cloth and wool dealers preferred to stick to their extremely decorative black and white, though the current scion of the Rowley family added a brick and stone extension to his father's beautiful timber-framed house. Otherwise the family mansions of the rising and enterprising middle class are a pattern of black and white: Ireland's Mansion and Owen's Mansion in Shrewsbury, the Llwyd Mansion in Oswestry, Bishop Percy's House in Bridgnorth – they had no intention of letting their names be forgotten. In the bishop's case the house came before him, for he was born there, and though at one time in his life he tried to prove he was descended from the Northumbrian Percys, his father was a well-to-do grocer of the town, and the bishop himself was educated at Bridgnorth Grammar School.

So the towns, by and large, retained the old, vertical timbering, which actually adapts very suitably to streetscape and shop-frontage, and admirably to taverns. In the country, with space and to spare, tastes differed widely. So did the provenance of the sites on which men built, often creating a palimpsest stretching back through the ages, and through two or three previous dwellings.

Here in Madeley, where I live, we have Madeley Court, now a hotel. It began life long ago as a grange of the priory of Wenlock, and the last prior retired to spend the last few years of his life here after the Dissolution. That argues one previous house at least, possibly more, since what was left of the one now restored dates from the early years of Elizabeth I. It seems to have been an extensive property the priory possessed here, possibly used and sanctioned as a chase for hunting, as Edward I certainly issued licence to the priory to enclose its wood of Madeley, and make a park there, though it was part of the royal forest. All the 'Park' names that occur here, Park Lane, Park Street, Park Avenue, Rough Park, have nothing to do with a modern public garden, and everything to do with a strictly guarded private enclosure. The house was well-supplied, it had a mill, and fishponds. After the prior's death in 1552 the Crown sold the property to Sir Robert Brook, and the house I knew in a ruinous state long ago was of his building. No mistake about the fishponds, they were there to be seen, but what the house had been in its heyday was hard to guess, for much of it was derelict, only a portion used as a farmhouse was habitable. Later, the local industry in decline shut in the house between pennystone mounds, which by my time had become very pleasant wooded hills. Thus framed, hidden away from the rest of Madeley, with the wilderness pools alongside, and the great skeleton house brooding over them, it was a very romantic and haunting place.

The gatehouse was the most complete part of the property at that time, a charming stone building with twin octagonal capped towers, though it was used then as cottages. Now it must be a ceremonial entrance once more, and the detritus of industrial wastes, become groves of sheltering trees again, contribute to the country aspect. Whatever metamorphoses are in store in the future, Madeley Court has proved itself durable enough to survive them.

Court and gatehouse are of stone, but at about this same time a thoroughly Elizabethan manor-house, E-shaped in compliment to the sovereign's initial, was being built in glorious half-timbering at Pitchford. It lies in that same triangle of country which holds Plaish, and, for that matter, three other major country houses, and several lesser ones. Dr Pevsner calls it, 'The most splendid piece of black-and-white building in Shropshire.' Again it was built by a wool merchant of Shrewsbury, Adam Otley, about 1560 to 1570. It lies low among gently rising green slopes, a meadow house, not attempting to dominate, making no pretence at having or simulating defences, utterly at ease in the confidence of its own charms. Never a car passes by the gate from which it can best be viewed at a distance, but pulls up to let its fascinated cargo get out to stare. Long and low, leaning along its gentle slope, supremely at rest and appropriate in its setting, under its great, gracious sweep of roof covering torso and wings, and topped by its garland of star-shaped chimneys, Pitchford would be hard to match. Its timbering is mainly vertical struts below, and diagonals and lozenges above, none of the really fanciful elaborations such as those in The Feathers at Ludlow. In such a long frontage it gains by its disciplined simplicity.

And this lovely house has a toy house of its own,

a timber-framed summer-house perched in the branches of a tree, a little higher up the garden slope. There must have been a family of children in the house when that was added to the amenities, probably early in the eighteenth century.

Ten years or so later the Corbet family were building on their ancestral lands some miles north-east of Shrewsbury. The distant view from the road of the grouping they left behind there is almost startling, certainly imposing, and it represents a history of the Corbets and the village of Moreton Corbet over many centuries. Like so many village churches, the one here, dedicated to St Bartholomew, shows clear evidence in its fabric and furnishings of every age since the Normans came: Norman chancel, fourteenth-century south aisle, west tower begun in the sixteenth and completed in the eighteenth century, Jacobean pulpit and lectern, eighteenth-century alterations and modern stained glass, and Corbet monuments from the sixteenth to the twentieth centuries.

The secular evidences are even more striking. In level, open fields the towering frontage of an Elizabethan mansion, crowned with tall ogee-shaped gables, and with the sky beyond showing clear through its large mullioned and transomed windows, comes as a considerable shock, even if the vision is splendid and the shock pleasurable.

Moreton Corbet is a shell, a transparency through which can be seen the sparse remnants of a somewhat older range, a very much older gatehouse, though somewhat altered when the main range was begun, and the remains of a castle keep dating back probably to about 1200. The family left no possibility of doubt as to the date of the magnificent house they were building in 1579, for that date is there to be read in one corner of the fabric, and 'E.R. 21' at the opposite corner, the twenty-first regnal year of Elizabeth I, which is 1579. She came to the throne in November 1557.

The design is clear, palatial but disciplined, and with such windows the finished house would have been full of light. But it never was finished. During the Civil War the county was divided in its loyalties, though mainly Royalist, and a great deal of minor skirmishing went on, with considerable damage to castles and manor-houses. Moreton Corbet was one of the victims. A Parliamentarian siege, war damage and fire left it the complex and majestic ruin it now is. A great deal of ambitious building was going on in Shropshire around 1580 to 1590, and Moreton Corbet would have been one of the most distinctive and personal designs of all had it been completed.

Broseley is the hilltop town above the Severn gorge where the ironmasters built their own stately homes later, and it still has the air of a place ambivalent between the rural and the industrial, and for that matter between the Georgian of the wealthy commercial masters and the Victorian of their employees. By no means the poorest and most pressured of employees, though, for Broseley, I fancy, has never in its history looked or felt very depressed. Still, it was, and still looks, the urban centre of the industrial revolution. Yet close to the edge of it, removed just far enough to have a completely rural outlook on all sides, and approached by a tree-lined lane with generous grass verges, lies my favourite among the Elizabethan houses of comfortable size, the kind everyone can imagine living in with pleasure. Mellow, warm, friendly and utterly beautiful, Benthall has every charm. The first time I ever visited it was on a bright summer day, and the whole house was full of sunlight. I always remember it so.

At the end of a country lane, church and house sit snugly together, the church having a back gate from the garden of the house. The older church was burned down in the Civil War, this one dates from 1667, and the house probably from about 1580, though earlier dates have been suggested. It is of warm creamy stone, with five gables in the frontage, and two big bay windows, one in the dining room, one at the dais end of the hall, both repeated on the floor above. Behind the house and to one side the ground rises, so that the garden climbs on that side by little paths and terraces, and trees fill in the backcloth to show up the golden stone at its best. On the other side the garden dips gently, and also in front of the house where the level drops to a long field, and further fields beyond. The chimney-stacks are clustered star-shapes, and snowy white fantails flutter from their dovecote to the roof and back again, with a bright eye on visitors with cameras, as though they are posing for photographs and have no intention of being overlooked. This is a house which has always been lived in and loved, and always by the same family, conditions which give it an inimitable repose and contentment.

Shipton Hall, in Corvedale, a few years younger than Benthall, is also built of a pleasant local stone, is similarly approachable in size and style, and has something of the same attractive domesticity about it. It is also very happily placed, at the top of a gentle slope beside the road, with its walled garden pleasantly disposed before it; and since the road is winding, from either direction this framed picture bursts on the eye with a shock of pleasure, house, handsome stable block at one side, dovecote behind, and shrubs and sweep of lawn enclosed but not hidden by the low stone wall. The house is H-shaped, the wings bolder at the front, but in the right-hand corner the entrance is contained within a square porch, which continues upward into a four-storey tower, taller than the gables of the roof and wings. Star-shaped brick chimney-stacks crown the roof. And as so often, the church keeps close company with the house, completing the picture at the left-hand rise of the garden front.

Condover, a few miles south of Shrewsbury on the Cound brook is a far more grandiose piece of work, but less appealing, at least to me. It was built by an Owen of Shrewsbury, who became one of Elizabeth I's judges. The house was not quite finished when he died in 1598. It is built of a light, creamy sandstone, with an E-plan frontage, and shorter wings at the back, large multi-lighted windows, mullioned and transomed, an imposing range of gables, and two short, square tower eminences at the junctions of wings and centre. Dr Pevsner considers it 'The grandest Elizabethan house in Shropshire'. I agree to admire it, but feel it is better suited to an institution than to a domestic dwelling. As indeed it has since been extremely apt and useful as an institution. The fate of the very large and very fine country houses, in a modern world in which large domestic staffs are things of the past, and expenses of maintenance constantly rise, presents as difficult a problem as that of redundant churches, far too lovely and valuable to be pulled down or left to rot, but tragically without a worthy function to keep them alive.

The Georgian houses in which the county is as rich as in Elizabethan ones, tend to be large indeed. I know them from photographs and by name, Cound, Buntingsdale, Mawley, Hawkstone, Longford – mostly red brick with stone dressings, occasionally stone, some with pillared porches, great towering, arrogant masses built to impress, and of an arbitrary symmetry to balance and temper the romantic manipulating of park and garden that came in with them, where rivers must be induced to flow where they could best be seen from the house, and provide a pleasing vista of bridge and meandering water, and the placing of every tree, as well as every grotto or temple, was a delicate decision, aimed at perfecting a composition as personal as a painting on canvas. But with only one of these am I intimately acquainted. For a number of years Attingham played a vital and unforgettable part in my life, and in the lives of thousands of other people.

During the war Attingham was occupied by the Army, but afterwards, when it came into the hands of the National Trust, it leased part of the accommodation to the projected Shropshire Adult College. In a time of idealism and optimism this idea had been launched with great enthusiasm. There were many vigorous branches of the Workers' Educational Association and similar

bodies, which looked forward eagerly to the
fulfilment of a dream, and, with backing from
county and borough and other bodies, the college
took shape in 1948. Naturally the state rooms,
though the music room was available for lectures
and concerts, were kept in the hands of the National
Trust and its professionals when it came to
redecoration and restoration, but parts which were
less vulnerable, the rooms which were to
accommodate weekend students, parts of the
courtyard and so on, were willing to welcome help
from hopeful amateurs, and working parties
mustered to help put the rooms in order prior to
opening. Sir George Trevelyan took over the duties
of warden, and set the tone of the enterprise, which
never flagged while he remained.

The first working party to spend a weekend
there, unloading the college beds and furnishings,
and painting, came from the Dawley branch of the
WEA, to which my brother and I belonged. I
missed it, as I was abroad for three months in the
summer of 1948, but I was there for the second
party, in September. In some ways those first weeks,
and the eventual opening, were the best days of all,
as anticipation is always particularly fine when you
are working personally for the end in view. Fees
were kept low so that entry should be open to as
wide an intake as possible, and under Sir George

Trevelyan's magnetic and passionate leadership the college began an exultant life. No one who has not been caught up heart and soul in such a co-operative enterprise can fully understand it, and those of us who have find difficulty in describing it.

To consider the setting first: the very lodge and main entrance gates of Attingham form part of a very remarkable crossroads group. Across the main road from the lodge lies the Mytton and Mermaid hotel, a fine eighteenth-century inn, with the church beyond it, and these adjoin the river Severn just where the road crosses it not by one bridge, but by two, for when the Georgian Atcham Bridge was built, the old one was left beside it, abandoned to the fishermen, and the visitor with time to spare, and in search of a good spot from which to photograph St Eata's church.

And within the enclosing walls, acres upon acres of park, with pools, fine trees and lawns, and the river Tern, which within the view from the house was diverted when Repton designed the gardens, to provide another very handsome bridge where the main road crosses. Lawns and a ha-ha before the frontage of the house, and cattle to provide life interest and detail in the pasture below. And across a footbridge from this formal apron, the deer park with miles of walks and herds of fallow deer.

The house itself dates from about 1785, eleven

bays wide, with an advanced portico on four Ionic
columns, and on either side curving colonnades
connecting the house with matching service wings,
one, the orangery, then being the warden's house.
These spread wings are what many of the other
massive, almost cubic Georgian houses lack, and
they give a very satisfying sense of grace and
stability. And the rooms inside are splendid. They
might be daunting, as the entire house might, to a
small group permanently domiciled there, but for a
houseful of very varied people met with one object
in mind, and busy getting to know one another
while they pursued the same objective, the set-up
was ideal.

And productive! There were courses on every
subject under the sun – music, painting, history,
ecology, architecture, literature, bird-song and wild
flowers, archaeology, astronomy. There were
concerts, plays, poetry, Shakespeare in the open air,
with the fac[ced]ade and the curving double
staircase to the doorway as backdrop, every kind of
stimulus to the mind and challenge to the skills,
sometimes skills never discovered before. I am
convinced that as people certainly learned to paint
at Attingham, so others learned to write, to think,
to develop the skills of the mind, and the talents
they never knew they possessed.

We still had occasional working parties, helping

wherever amateurs could usefully be deployed. Odd things I remember: one of our own local members painting in the courtyard, at the top of a ladder braced close to the open double doors of the yard, leaning too far to one side, and having the presence of mind to dive for the top of the wooden doors, and even to yell 'Timber!' in warning to those working below, as the ladder heeled away from under him. He was rescued without damage. And there was at this unobtrusive rear side of the house a ladder of iron rungs fixed to the wall, by which it was possible to climb up to the roof, and over into the deep leaded channel within the parapet, and walk along to the pediment at the porch. Somewhere I have mislaid my small copy of the photograph Sir George once took, and which in the log book of Attingham was captioned 'The Pargeters on the Pediment'. Later someone took thought, and banned the climb to the roof, fearful of accidents, but the fixed ladder was stable enough, and there was no real danger.

Unfortunately everything which is dazzlingly successful has its enemies, people who do not want such facilities for themselves, or are afraid to venture into the water, and begrudge them to those who do want them, and are not afraid. There began to be murmurs that public money should not subsidize such a college, and pressure to make the fees sustain the service in full, which would have meant putting courses out of the reach of those who might most benefit from them. In the end Attingham was forced to close because official support was withdrawn. We had one final day of demonstrating what had been achieved, in poetry, art, music and the burning appetite for learning, and then we separated, I hope to spread the same spirit as individuals. Certainly I know that those years at Attingham opened windows upon an immensely expanded world for very many people, and I am sure nothing put into that co-operative has been wasted, or fallen without fruit.

Stokesay Castle
Probably the finest example of a thirteenth-century fortified manor house in the country.

Bromfield
Gatehouse to the Benedictine Priory founded in 1155, the only other remains being the
church of St Mary which is much altered.

Wenlock Priory
The site of a nunnery founded in the seventh century and later developed as a Cluniac Priory,
has some impressive remains dating from the twelfth century.

Shrewsbury Abbey

A Benedictine abbey of the eleventh century, with the fourteenth-century refectory pulpit in the foreground.

Lilleshall Abbey
Started in the twelfth century, these remains give a very good indication of the grand scale of
Norman monastic buildings.

Stretton Hills
Wonderful walking country each side of an old Roman road which ran through the valley at
Church Stretton.

Ludlow Castle
The eleventh-century castle at Ludlow dominates a crossing of the River Teme.

Moreton Corbet

A Norman chancel in the church, the remains of a twelfth-century castle and the burnt out
shell of an Elizabethan hall create an interesting group.

SIX

LOCAL HEROES, NATIVE AND STRANGER

Of illustrious Salopians there are plenty, and of varied and surprising talents. Some distinct oddities among them, like the very, very, very old man, Thomas Parr, whose genius was for living life to the full well past his century. His fame rests not so much upon the hundred and fifty-three years he is reputed to have reached, but for the way those years were employed. For, according to the records, he left it until he was eighty to notice the opposite sex and marry one of them, which argues a rather late developer; but once having got the idea, he ventured on an affair outside marriage at the age of one hundred, fathered a child, and went on to embark on a second marriage at one hundred and twenty-two, after ten years as a widower. There is nothing on record of what the two Mrs Parrs felt about the matter, which is a pity.

There is no need to take the old fellow's account of his years too seriously, since his birth was not registered; but he must have been genuinely ancient, since his neighbours and contemporaries had at least the evidence of their own eyes and their parents' memories as to how long he had been extant. There are, of course, better claims to fame than simply doing penance in church at a hundred years old, or even seventy, for getting a girl with child. Still, after its fashion it is certainly an achievement.

About the best-known of Shropshire's celebrities much has been written, and most people are familiar, for instance, with the names of our most famous warriors: John Talbot, Earl of Shrewsbury, who admittedly was a very tough and brave fighter, but showed no chivalry towards Joan of Arc; Clive, who carved out an empire in India with surprising ease when you read the tale of his battles; Rowland, Lord Hill, Wellington's Quartermaster-General and right-hand man throughout the Peninsula war. Sir Herbert Edwardes, of the Edwardes family of Frodesley, is perhaps less known; for his army career in India he earned the name of the hero of Multan, though I have never discovered exactly what happened to attach his name to that particular place; but he must have been an able diplomat as well, since his chief claim to fame is that he persuaded Afghanistan to remain neutral and not clamber on to the bandwagon during the Mutiny, by which feat he must surely have saved a considerable number of lives both British and Indian.

Our chief seaman, too, needs no new panegyrics. Benbow met with the usual difficulties of a sailor rising from the lower deck and a middle-class background to outshine at all points the gentlemen, almost amateurs, who considered the higher appointments in the service as their peculiar province, theirs by right, and who deeply resented Benbow's well-deserved promotion over their heads. One point in James II's favour is that he knew a good seaman when he found one, and cared not at all about his humble beginnings. As one of our naval historian officers at Western Approaches said, in one of the lectures we hounded him into delivering, 'James was a very good admiral, and then he came to the throne, and proved an absolutely bum king.'

The story of Sarah Hoggins, of Bolas Magna, who married her father's lodger, known locally for his bearing and speech as 'Gentleman Harry', and found herself eventually Marchioness of Exeter, is equally well known. Tennyson, apparently unable to conceive that a village beauty should be quite capable of rising to such an occasion, makes her wilt away to her death under:

. . . the burden of an honour
Unto which she was not born.

Actually she died in childbirth with her fourth child, and I believe and hope that during the all too brief years of her elevation to the peerage she thoroughly enjoyed the social life of Burghley House. After all, she knew her husband well by the time he inherited. Their first child was born, died young, and is buried in Great Bolas; this and other vicissitudes they had weathered together, it would take more than the shock of finding herself a marchioness to make her heart fail now.

Nor does our very local hero, Matthew Webb, who was born at Dawley and learned to swim in the river at Ironbridge, need any introduction. His name rises irresitibly out of the rapids below Niagara every time a new Channel swimmer pares another quarter-of-an-hour from the time he took on that first successful Channel swim. No matter how they have improved on his time in the hundreds of crossings since then, there could be only one first, and that belonged to Captain Matthew Webb.

There are Shropshire firsts in the field of medicine, too. William Withering, born in Wellington, was the first to investigate the use of digitalis in treating heart diseases. He was also an early campaigner for the abolition of the slave trade. And at Bromfield there was Henry Hickman, who fought throughout his short life to convince the medical profession that pain could be banished by the use of anaesthetics in surgery. Unfortunately nobody listened to him, and only years after his death, when others were treading the same experimental paths, did someone remember his claims, and give him the credit due.

Concerning poets, we can range from Langland — even though some authorities dispute Cleobury Mortimer's claim to be his birthplace — through Newport's Thomas Brown, the wit who satirized the pretentious and delighted the irreverent in the seventeenth century, and in four lines, known to everybody, made Dr Fell famous for not being loved; to the brothers Lord Herbert of Cherbury and George Herbert the divine, both excellent poets, and finally to Wilfred Owen, certainly the finest poet of the First World War.

We have our divines also, in the Puritan Richard Baxter, who had experience of both sides in the Civil War, and was disillusioned, ultimately, with both. And Bishop Heber. And Adam Grafton, who was parish priest at Withington, Dean of the college of St Mary's at Shrewsbury, and then a cleric at court, chaplain to the unhappy little king, Edward V, murdered in the Tower, and later, as if one such tragic memory was not enough for any man, chaplain also to Henry VII's eldest son Arthur, who died at sixteen and left Catherine a young widow at Ludlow.

The name of the first Lord Acton of Aldenham Hall, scholar and historian, would get a place in most lists of the county's notable sons. His ancestors were made baronets for their loyalty to the Stuart cause. But how about Lord Acton's grandfather, the sixth baronet, who gets overlooked most of the time? He seems to me to merit a mention in any *Who's Who*. Sir John Acton mounted an expedition against the Barbary corsairs, in which he is reputed to have delivered no less than four thousand Spanish prisoners from slavery. Then he joined the household of Ferdinand IV, King of Naples, at whose court Sir William Hamilton was British ambassador. This was when the Napoleonic Wars were in full career, and Nelson was with a fleet in the Mediterranean because Napoleon had gone to Egypt. Naples was an uneasy neutral, the position of the royal family none too secure, since the king was Spanish and his queen Austrian, the sister, in fact, of Marie Antoinette, and neither of them was particularly popular. There was a French army in Italy, Naples was not too anxious to provoke an attack. In this curious kingdom Acton was Prime Minister and head of both army and navy, such as they were.

The triumph of Aboukir Bay, the Battle of the Nile, relieved Europe of its most extreme fear of Napoleon for the time being, and Nelson returned to Naples with his ships in the full flood of victory, and there urged the king to come out openly against the French. But the first encounter between the Neapolitan army and the French army in Italy proved disastrous, succeeding only in provoking a campaign against Naples. Finally Acton, in co-operation with the Hamiltons and Nelson, recommended that the royal family should withdraw to Sicily, and played a large part in helping them to get aboard ship secretly, and with all the most valuable of their movable goods, before the French arrived. In Nelson's ships, and picking up other refugees along the way, they sailed in wretched weather for Palermo, Acton along with them. Lady Hamilton, it seems, was as good a sailor as she was a diplomat in a crisis, and proved a tower of strength aboard when almost everyone else but the crew was seasick.

This Neopolitan incident, of course, was the beginning of the love affair that rocked Europe. Nelson came wounded from victory at the Nile back to the flattering attentions of a woman who was not merely beautiful, but had proved herself an able assistant in managing difficult international relations, and who seems to have been completely fearless when things grew dangerous. Small wonder if this experience of working together under stress, and feeling complete reliance each on the other, cemented a passion which had begun without reservations, and continued so ever after.

Sir John Acton remained in Palermo with the royal family, at least for some time. What further adventures befell him I have no idea, but he seems hardly the type to have subsided gracefully into a quiet life. His grandson the historian apparently disapproved of his grandsire, for he refused his fortune, regarding it as ill-gotten, though whether in connection with the Barbary raid or the smuggling of royal money out of Naples is not stated. It seems to me that anyone who contrived to release four thousand prisoners, of whatever nationality, from the galleys of the Barbary Coast is entitled to do a little piracy of his own in the process.

We can claim, of course, one other supreme historian. His father came over in the retinue of Earl Roger de Montgomery, being a clerk in his household, took an English wife, and had three children. It was he who encouraged his lord to take over the building and establishment of Shrewsbury Abbey. Orderic Vitalis, afterwards a monk of St Evroult, was almost certainly born in or near Shrewsbury, for quite certainly he was baptized at St Eata's church at Atcham. His *Ecclesiastical History* is the best of all the contemporary chronicles of the late eleventh and early twelfth centuries. He explained the title by saying that he had set out to write the history of the Christian people in his time, and he kept his chronicle for half a century, closing it only when he felt near his death. When that time came he ended with a wonderful and moving farewell to the world, in which he makes his own personal statement of faith.

'Lo, I, borne down by age, seek to close this my book.' So his testament begins.

I was baptised on the sabbaeth of Easter, at Attingesham, a village of England, seated upon the great river Severn. There, by the ministry of Ordric the priest, didst Thou, O my God, beget me anew, by water and the Holy Ghost, and gavest unto me the name of my godfather, the aforesaid priest. Thence, at the age of five years, was I sent to school in the city of Scrobesbury: and offered unto Thee the first services of my clergyhood in the church of Saint Peter and Saint Paul the apostles. There did Siguard, a famous priest, teach me, for the space of five years, the rudiments of the Latin tongue, and instructed me in psalms and hymns, and other necessary parts of education. In the mean time, Thou didst exalt the aforesaid church, which belonged to my father, and which was situate on the river Mole, and didst erect the venerable Abbey, through the pious devotion of Roger the Earl.

It was Thy pleasure to remove me from Thy service in that spot, and to take me from my kinsfolk, lest the ties of blood, which are so often an hindrance to Thy servants, might estrange my affections from the observance of Thy laws, to the lusts of the flesh. Therefore, O God of glory, Thou who of old didst command Abraham to remove out of his country and from his kindred, didst in like wise inspire my father, Odelerius, wholly to renounce me, for Thy Love, and to resign me entirely to Thee. Many were the tears which he shed, when he delivered me, a weeping infant, to the charge of Rainald the monk, banishing me for ever from my native land. Nor did he ever see me from that moment. Instead of my native land, and the caresses of a tender father, he promised unto me, on Thy part, the joys of paradise. Do Thou, O God of Sabaoth, receive his prayers, and grant those his petitions.

Thus, at the age of ten years, did I cross the British sea; unknowing and unknown I arrived in Normandy. Like Joseph, I heard a strange language. Yet, under Thy protection, I experienced all the gentle offices of humanity at the hands of foreigners. In the eleventh year of my age I was admitted a monk in the monastery of Uticum, by the venerable abbot Mainer, and on Sunday the 21st day of September received the tonsure, after the manner of clerks. At the same time, instead of my English name, which sounded harsh in their ears, they called me Vitalis, in allusion to one of Saint Maurice's companions, whose feast fell on that day.

In this abbey have I, by Thy favour, dwelt for fifty-six years, loved and respected by my brethren and companions far beyond my deserts. I have borne the heat and cold, and the burden of the day, among Thy labourers in the vineyard of Sorech, securely expecting the penny, my wages; for Thou art faithful that hast promised. Six abbots, Thy vicars, as my fathers and masters have I reverenced: to wit, Mainer and Serlo, Roger and Warin, Richard and Ralph, who presided over the convent of Uticum, as men who were aware that they must render an account of the souls committed to their charge.

At the age of sixteen, on the 15th of March, I was ordained sub-deacon by Gilbert, bishop of Lisieux, at the instance of Serlo, abbot elect. Two years after, on the 26th of March, Serlo bishop of Seez invested me with the stole of deacon; in which order I cheerfully served Thee by the space of fifteen years. At length, when I had arrived at my thirty-third year, William archbishop of Rouen loaded me with the burden of priesthood on the new year's day. At the same time he ordained two hundred and forty-four deacons and one hundred and twenty priests, with whom I approached Thy altar in the Holy Spirit, and have now fulfilled Thy sacred ministry for thirty-four years, with readiness and fidelity.

Thus, thus, O Lord God, Thou who didst fashion me, and didst breathe into my nostrils the breath of life, hast Thou, through these various gradations, imparted to me Thy gifts, and formed my years to Thy service. In all the places to which Thou hast led me, Thou hast caused me to be beloved, by Thy bounty, not by my own deserving. For all Thy benefits, O merciful Father, I thank Thee, I laud and bless Thee; for my numberless offences, with tears I implore Thy mercy. For the praise of Thy unwearied goodness, look upon Thy creature, and blot out all my sins. Grant me the will to persist in Thy service, and strength to withstand the attacks of Satan, till I attain, by Thy grace, the inheritance of everlasting life. And what I have prayed for myself, I pray, O God, for my friends and well-doers. The same also I pray for all the faithful; and forasmuch as the efficacy of our own merits cannot suffice to obtain those eternal gifts, after which the desires of the perfect aspire.

O Lord God, Almighty Father, Creator and Ruler of the Angels, Thou true Hope and eternal Blessedness of the righteous, may the glorious intercession of the Holy Virgin and Mother, Mary, and all the Saints, aid us in Thy sight, with the merits of Our Lord Jesus Christ, Redeemer of all men, who liveth and reigneth with Thee in the unity of the Holy Ghost; world without end. Amen.

I have tried, sometimes, to write like that. Anyone who could write like that, and sound like that even in translation, is worth a very high place among the memorable. Even the translation, early nineteenth century, carried the *History of Shrewsbury* by Owen and Blakeway well into the field of pure literature, in addition to the other merits of their masterwork.

As a postscript, and I hope not an anticlimax, but a gentle diminuendo with a grace of its own, like the reconciliation at the end of a passionate novel, let me mention Robert More, of the village and family of More, a keen botanist and friend of Linnaeus. With another friend, the Duke of Atholl, he entered into a friendly race to bring back from the Tyrol the first larches ever to be planted in Britain. Robert More won. He got his trees into the ground at home one day ahead of the duke, and in the park of Linley Hall there are still larches descended from the first ever to flourish in England. Not a bad claim to fame, at a time when so many species, both of flora and fauna, are being hounded towards oblivion.

There are a number of our local heroes who are not really ours, like A.E. Housman, born over the border in a neighbouring county, but by his own act in choosing the title he did for his poems for ever associated with Shropshire, and welcome here, for his poetry is some of the most purely singable ever written, as generations of composers testify by their settings. There is the Reverend William Fletcher of Madeley, born Guillaume de la Fléchère, who came from Switzerland as tutor to one of the Hill family after a brief military career, and became the saint of the coal field and the ironworks as vicar of Madeley and friend of Wesley.

And there is Sir Philip Sidney, sometime pupil at the old Shrewsbury School which is now the Library, with his friend lifelong, Fulke Greville, and now the patron and ideal of the present school. His father being Lord President of the Council of the Marches, Philip spent a good part of his boyhood in residence at Ludlow castle, as well as his years at school here. And like everyone else, everyone in his own time who came within reach of his personal charm, we reckon we have a just claim to consider him ours at least by adoption, or as a loved and visiting cousin.

Shrewsbury is twinned with Zutphen in the Netherlands, the town where was fought the battle in which Sidney got his death-wound. A few years ago I was asked to contribute a short piece to a commemorative volume to be presented to the burgomaster of Zutphen on his retirement, from the borough of Shrewsbury. I hope my Dutch friends will let me borrow it back to quote here:

I do not know, and have never thought to enquire, who first conceived the idea of twinning towns in different countries, but clearly his intent was to promote international friendship, and enable people on both sides to get to know and respect each other, to the ultimate end that world peace should at least have its chance, however remote, to inherit the earth.

Clearly such a relationship between towns has an added significance if it is based on a positive historical link between the chosen pair. Our link with Zutphen could hardly be more illustrious or appropriate. A little over four hundred years ago England sent the best it had to assist the patriots in the Netherlands in their struggle to throw off the dominance of Spain. Brought up at Ludlow, educated at Shrewsbury in the old school, forerunner of the present one that stands high above the Severn, Sir Philip Sidney went out to become governor of Flushing, and to get his death-wound at the battle of Zutphen, where a small company of fifty Dutch and English allies waited in the thick mist of morning to intercept a Spanish provision convoy, expecting only a nominal escort, only to find, as the fog suddenly lifted, that they faced about three thousand Spanish troops. They made three charges against this army, and each time broke its line. Sidney had his thigh shattered by a bullet, and was carried off the field to endure days of progressive agony, we are told 'with heroic courage and sweetness of temper', before he died of his wounds.

What happened as he was being carried away, everybody knows. There can never have been any drink, not the nectar of the Gods, not the hemlock of Socrates, half so famous as that cup of cold water that Sidney relinquished to a dying soldier, because 'thy need is yet greater than mine'. It did not save either the nobleman who gave it or the lowly soldier who received it, but it expressed the best side of the aristocratic principle, and it grew into an icon, a grail to pursue in the world's slow and lame advance towards the perfectibility of humankind.

Not a bad symbol, to be the link between Shrewsbury and Zutphen. Especially as we English, like you Netherlanders, still remember shared heroisms of the last war, and recognise the historic continuity four hundred years old, and still unbroken. Long may it continue!

It is clear that Philip has the hold on me that he seems to have had on everyone who ever came into his orbit, let alone into his living presence. He occupies, in the gorgeous procession of Elizabethan grandees, the unique position of Sir Lancelot in the Arthurian knighthood, an irresistible magnet attracting the love of both men and women equally, and earning it by a special quality of courtesy and consideration in particular to the humble and helpless. What happened on the field of Zutphen was no solitary gesture, no gesture at all, it came naturally to him.

When he died, all England went into mourning. William Byrd's funeral song for him laments the age's loss:

> Come to me, grief, for ever,
> Come to me tears, day and night,
> Come to me plaint, ah, helpless,
> Just grief, heart's tears, plaint worthy.
> Go fro me dread to die now,
> Go fro me, care to live more,
> Go fro me joys all on earth,
> Sidney, O Sidney is dead!

And Fulke Greville, his lifelong companion and friend, wrote of him:

> Knowledge his light hath lost, Valour hath slain her knight,
> Sidney is dead, dead is my friend, dead is the world's delight.

And in course of time, when he himself followed, he left as his own epitaph: 'Servant to Queen Elizabeth, Counsellor to King James, and friend to

Sir Philip Sidney.' What further could be said? And there was never, as far as I know, a single envious voice, even, to attempt slander against his excellence.

There is also, of course, Thomas Telford, come down from Dumfriesshire to strike roots in our soil. But of him, or of his twentieth-century namesake, more hereafter.

SEVEN

NEW HORIZONS

In the optimistic years after the war the germ of an idea emerged, from a group of councillors elected to what was then Dawley Urban District Council, which has produced a major change in the topography and nature of Shropshire. I called it a county without cities, but something which may yet become a city is growing up here in the region of the old industrial iron and steel country. Telford New Town is a reality, a growing and energetic entity, though composed of a number of smaller towns which preserve all they can of their own individuality.

The name came later. The initiative I remember very well, since I lived with and noted the discussions from the very beginning. My brother was one of the councillors concerned. The subject of placing New Towns to the general advantage in the regions was much in the air, and a very good case could be made for founding one here in a district which had pioneered the Industrial Revolution, and was now in total decline as the

result of being so early in the field that its natural
resources had been bled away and one-third of its
territory was reduced to pennystone clay and
industrial spoilheaps. I remember the many
discussions, the planning, the marshalling of
forensic argument, before a deputation from
Dawley Council, including my brother, and
accompanied by the officials, clerk and surveyor (I
think both of them, but certainly one) went up to
London, met the Wrekin MP at the House of
Commons, and had an interview with the Minister.

Some years went by after that before anything
began to happen, but from that time on the project
of Dawley New Town was on the table and under
positive consideration. The inititative came from
Dawley Urban District Council, not from
Westminster.

The arguments they mustered for the visit were
basically these:

1. The very fact that one-third of the Dawley area was
spoiled land meant that the very minimum of
agricultural land need be taken up, whereas waste
mounds could be levelled for building without loss
and to advantage.

2. The area was in depression precisely because it had
been the first in the field, when safeguards for
restoration did not exist, and had suffered

accordingly. It was a justifiable claim that some reparation was due, and a New Town would bring revival to a deprived population.

3. There was an acknowledged need for industry of some kind to move into central Wales, but it was unreasonable to expect overcrowded areas like the Birmingham conurbation to make a leap of eighty miles west, without proper provision for transport and some likelihood of success. But if the move of forty miles or so to Dawley could be made, and the New Town firmly established and properly serviced with roads or rail or both, then later light industry might well find it feasible to go the other few miles into Wales.

4. Depressed though our area was, the skills necessary to industry were still there, traditional and waiting to be employed. A work-force ready and willing.

That was how it began, not imposed from a distance, but invited in. It is true that when it began to show signs of becoming a reality the plans had been greatly changed in Whitehall, and not everyone approved of the changes. Instead of remaining Dawley New Town, envisaging an ultimate population of 90,000 and abstaining from taking in more good farmland than was inevitable to achieve that size, it had been taken across the A5 and swollen to include Madeley, Ironbridge and Coalbrookdale, Oakengates and Wellington, with a population up to 150,000. As Dawley New Town it had been officially promulgated in 1963. Five years later it was the larger concept that became Telford.

Had it remained as originally conceived, it would have also remained Dawley. But with five towns of strong local character involved, it is understandable that the name became a delicate point, and if it was essential to avoid the possible competition and recriminations and choose a name from elsewhere, I think they did pretty sensibly in making use of Telford. Thomas was, after all, our county surveyor from 1788 to his death in 1834, and did reasonably well by the county, apart from driving the A5 clean through the cloister of Shrewsbury Abbey. His bridges, churches and roads are here to be seen, and of quality, and it was no fault of his if St Chad's fell down because his advice was not taken. And Telford sounds like a town, is brief and clear.

The first manifestations, however, had a very strange effect. The first housing estate, at Sutton Hill, took shape fairly rapidly, but presented some forms in housing so unusual as to be difficult to accept. Roofs, for instance, gouged into a deep valley throughout their lengths, a perfect repository for lost footballs and cricket balls, moss, grass and dead leaves. The beginnings of the intended town centre followed. A pale modern growth of buildings sprang up in the middle of nowhere, surrounded on all sides and for considerable distances by open fields and hedges, and with one projecting, tent-like roof in the midst. It looked for all the world like a caravanserai encamped for the night, and continued to look like that for a long time, as though the next morning it might have struck camp and moved on to the next oasis in this green rural desert.

Given the choice of site, anything newly planted there would have been alien. It takes time and patience to assimilate things virtually from outer space, especially when the old inhabitants have to witness the removal of the familiar before the unfamiliar can be installed. Huge scars lacerated the greenness round us, tearing open the ground designated for the housing estates. Close to home I witnessed the removal of the nearby farm, within days simply obliterated. Huge earth-moving machines proliferated, ripping up the paths that were our dog-walks. No wonder if most people suffered doubts and regrets. But the most remarkable thing about such drastic changes of scene is the rapidity with which the old contours are completely forgotten, and neither mind nor eye can recall them, or reconstruct with any clarity what has been demolished.

The second estate, Woodside, was more rational;

compact, contained within a perimeter road, and so arranged as to vary the angles and provide a degree of privacy. People came in freely and from many regions to occupy the houses. The difficulty of starting from scratch at welding into a community has no easy solution, and for a while each estate in turn suffered a derogatory reputation, whether deserved or undeserved, before it settled down into the rhythm of living. The first small industrial estate, at Tweedale, struck me as being somehow more attractive and well laid out than the housing quarters, and remains pleasing still. The big industrial factory sites opened up quite imposing prospects, with some handsome buildings and plenty of air and space. And around and about all this development a great new road system curved and twined, some of it motorway standard, the rest not far behind, with roundabouts scattered like sequins at every intersection.

For a matter of years, filling the houses and flats was easier than inducing industry to come in and provide the jobs. Some of the firms that did come early withdrew again, some of the smaller ones failed and closed down. But gradually confidence and capital did begin to find its way in here, and once started and running, the process proved cumulative, and the pace accelerated. The town centre became indeed the centre of a colossal flower, the stems of which were roads and the petals increasingly ambitious and confident buildings, shops, office blocks, recreation centres, cinema, restaurants and hotels.

From the beginning, the Development Corporation did some most imaginative and reconciling things. It raised in nurseries and planted out throughout the territory thousands of trees, and millions of bulbs. It was a popular trip for denizens of the Birmingham conurbation, in spring, to drive round the new, wide-shouldered roads of Telford to view the golden blaze of daffodils all along the verges and on every island. It also set out to beautify every corner of the centre complex with hanging baskets of flowers and every kind of stone container planned in careful colourings. The real triumph came in 1990, when Telford outshone all rivals to become, first, Britain's Town of Flowers, and finally the European Town of Flowers. No one who saw the displays along the Wharfage at Ironbridge, or in the Civic Square at the Town Centre, where Telford, above lifesize, leans on the 'O' of his own name to enjoy the prospect of water and flowers before him, can be in any doubt that the award was well deserved.

Growth continues. As fast as new industrial estates spring up, their available factories seem to be filled. It has taken a long time, but Telford is an established fact, and an important one. And the several Japanese firms which have come and settled here have put a great deal of goodwill and generosity into contributing to, as well as exploiting, the town they have adopted. The town park, many beautiful acres of it, owes its cherry garden to their interest. One advantage of the ground about the centre is that it undulates gently, in a way that provides several levels to the park, and some very fine views, as well as intimate, closed corners screened from the world. I have not visited the children's Wonderland, but my youngest informants are enthusiastic, and certainly hundreds of children do make good use of its many amenities, the castle, the gingerbread house, and other delightful things.

Concerning the architecture of the buildings in the centre there must be almost as many opinions as viewers. Several of the largest office blocks are startling in their setting, but I have no objection to being startled if the shock is pleasurable, or even stimulating, and in the changing light of the day some of these giants seem to me constantly more approachable and appropriate than I first thought them, with some of the qualities of monumental sculpture, such as nature suddenly confronts us with in mountain country. There are many kinds of beauty. Proportion and balance are the essentials, colour is a versatile elaboration. There is one block in the centre which makes highly dramatic use of blue. That one I begin to think beautiful, even if it is in the manner of a stage set for *The Shape of Things to Come*.

The one fine thing which, most of all, we owe to the New Town of Telford is the creation of the Ironbridge Gorge Museum. Without the backing of the town, and the intelligent realization that the gorge could be its greatest asset, such a project could never have been launched. But since its inception in 1967 it has continued to grow and to attract not only summer visitors but world attention. The Development Corporation had the foresight to insist on the inclusion of both banks of the river in its territory, in order to be able to control development there, and protect the environment. All the overgrown furnace sites and relics of industrial buidlings were cleared, the bridge itself refurbished, the original furnace in the Coalbrookdale works excavated and protected, and the full scope of the museum spread over six major exhibits and many smaller ones. There is the Coalbrookdale Museum of Iron on the old works grounds, with the original furnace; the former warehouse and wharf by the river, which does duty as a Visitor Centre and special exhibition concerned with the Severn; the Coalport China Museum; the tile works at Jackfield; Rosehill House, the home of the Darbys in the eighteenth century; and above all, the Blist's Hill Open Air Museum, with the remaining stretch of the canal and the inclined plane down to Coalport, the engine-houses and the coalmine which belonged to the site itself, and many nineteenth-century items which have been brought here. The valley that is the home of all this, going down from Madeley to the Severn at Coalport, happens also to be very beautiful in itself, a suitable setting and a fair introduction to the grander beauty of the gorge below.

The staff used to have an annual charcoal burn, perhaps still do, among many other activities. When I had a solid fuel Aga I used to buy my charcoal from the museum, and very good stuff it was, much better than the commercial product in the hardware shops.

In 1978 the Ironbridge Gorge Museum was named as the European Museum of the Year. Who knows what other laurels this district may pick up in the future?

One very strange and momentous find was added to the amenities of Shropshire and the wonders of the world in September of 1986, when excavations to enlarge a sand and gravel quarry, being worked by the firm of ARC Western, at Condover, uncovered some very large bones. Experts were called in, and on their advice further search in the same excavation produced several more bones to confirm that here was a discovery of much more than local importance. What the contractor's machines had uncovered proved positively to be the remains of an adult mammoth about twenty-five to thirty years old, together with the bones of two baby mammoths. Later, with the discovery of more bones this estimate was increased to three babies. The remains were embedded in a field of very heavy dark-blue clay, and it seemed that all the victims must have become trapped as in a morass, and been unable to struggle free. The thought of such a long and lingering death for any creature is moving enough. The subsequent temporary exhibition set up at RAF Cosford, brilliantly composed and lit, with a full-size reconstruction of the mammoth and of one of the small ones, realistically posed and beginning to sink in the soft clay, made the fate of the victims even more shattering by the addition of sound, the bellowing of the adult, and the screams of the baby. It was a *tour de force*, so much so that many people found it deeply disturbing. Still, to raise the deaths of creatures nearly thirteen thousand years removed from us to the level of tragedy, and make modern humankind feel it as such, is perhaps right and salutary. Even pity thousands of years after the event may not be too late, if time is a unity.

EIGHT

MIRROR IMAGE

Throughout my life my home base has never been more than three miles from the village where I was born. To set out from here towards the ends of the earth is a fine thing, provided I go with unshaken certainty that in due course I shall be coming back. Nor for every man is it essential that this indispensible place which is home should be also his birthplace; some of the spots that prove beloved over all are found, and chosen, and prove just as valid. But for most of us the earth and air on which we first open our eyes are those where our hearts fix and determine. Some of us, in a world too often divided, find a second dwelling as dear as the original, but I am not sure that is a happy fate. The old proverb says: He is homeless who has two homes.

The interplay between man and his environment affects the way he lives his life, the work he does and the way he does it. And Shropshire has left its images in my books as indelibly as in my memory and imagination. I am well aware that my writing is very visual, I paint in words. The landscape, the townscape, weather and season are all there within and between the lines. There are no precise factual portraits, such as I have attempted when writing, for instance, about scenes which have excited and delighted me in India, trying, I suppose, to show them to readers just as I saw them, and convey to them that excitement and delight. Shropshire is present as a pervasive sense of place, never fully revealed, but strongly felt. Only now and then have I used a recognizable place, and even then the copy is not photographic. In the case of the historical novels it cannot be, even imagination falling short when it comes to envisaging the changes over the centuries, but when writing history, even in the form of fiction, every documented and ascertainable fact must be respected, and an effort made to present events and locations as truly as possible.

Thus in *A Bloody Field by Shrewsbury* I tried to describe the battle and the battlefield with strict precision, just as I tried to portray the three embattled Henrys as a great deal of reading and thinking had made me see them. I had that book in my mind, and indeed on my mind, for ten years before I began to write it. It was one of the most bitter and destructive clashes on English ground, and it happened in my native county. I could not let it slip away without examining fully the circumstances that led up to it, and the consequences that followed it. Nor without going back to the church and loitering within it and without, and thinking about the warriors now dust underneath their memorial.

The Heaven Tree and its sequels took me over a good part of western Shropshire in a roving refresher course, especially along the Roman road on the flank of the Long Mountain, with the Breiddens looming at the northern end of the ridge, and a grand, stormy view of the river valley, the meadows that hold all that remains of Strata Marcella, and the town of Welshpool. This was still history, even though the fictional story woven into it took pride of place, so all that was historical had to be exact. But the castle that never existed I could place where I chose, provided I took care to account for its absence at the end.

This is my favourite of all my work, the one that comes nearest to what I wanted it to be.

The novels of Brother Cadfael, centred round the monastic life of Shrewsbury's Benedictine abbey in the twelfth century, obviously adhere, as completely as possible, to what is known of the house and the town at that time. We have been very lucky in preserving the Cartulary of the abbey to be edited and published in full, as well as possessing a number of fine antiquarian works on the town and the county. Every tiny, detailed fact discovered adds to the pleasure of writing about places well known lifelong and well loved. In these books the topography is as true as I can make it, with some speculation on the changes the centuries have made.

But even in the modern suspense novels, which claim the privileges of imaginative fiction, Shropshire is very much a presence, on my mind and emerging from my mind, to colour and haunt the background in shadow while my characters move in the light of the foreground. Sometimes its influence is clear and strong, as in the Aurae Phiala of *City of Gold and Shadows*, which is a projection, though not a portrait, of Uriconium, and was certainly suggested by that haunting and haunted city. With that in mind, it would not be difficult to locate the fishing inn I christened The Salmon's Return, in the same book, though I never consciously copied its pleasant appearance and proximity to the Severn.

As for the imaginary, yet by no means imaginary, county I have called Midshire, with its capital at Comerbourne, the county of all the novels concerning the Felse family, what could it be but Shropshire, with its border ambivalence and western frontier of mysterious hills? I had more than one Shropshire hill in mind when I described the Hallowmount, in *Flight of a Witch*. It is a little too gentle for the antediluvian lizard-length of the Stiperstones, but has something of the same menace, which is no menace to the natives. They, like the sixth-formers in the book, born among the slightly uncanny and on familiar terms with it, find 'nothing incongruous in having one foot in the twentieth century and one in the roots of time.' I think the Callow probably comes closest to the image.

The Follymead of *Black is the Colour of My Truelove's Heart* is certainly not Attingham, though it is presented as a weekend college bringing together households of very varied people for courses of lectures on equally varied subjects, in this case traditional and folk-song. Follymead's bizarre architecture bears no resemblance to Attingham's classic grandeur, nor are there any portraits among the students gathered for the occasion. But undoubtedly the pleasure and the profit I derived from Attingham's memorable weekends, and the gratitude I felt for it, suggested the book, and it was written with affection.

Still in Midshire, though perilously near the border, indeed straying over it, the Middlehope of *The Knocker on Death's Door* and *Rainbow's End* is quite decidedly the upper Teme valley, though the village names I have used won't be found there. The scenery will, the widening valley and diminishing stream as the road climbs, the bare grassy watershed before the descent into Wales, possibly even a heron standing in the little pool before the road dips again. The valley appears first in *The Knocker on Death's Door*, when George Felse, coming back from the Welsh coast, chooses to make use of it rather than the main roads on his way home. And I have taken a liberty here by transferring to the valley road a feature that belongs elsewhere.

Road and river wound inextricably along the valley, crossing and re-crossing in an antique dance of their own. In some of those bridges there was Roman masonry. There was even a short stretch of Roman causeway still exposed at the approach to one of them, perhaps twelve yards of huge stones laid like crazy paving, none too smooth even now, after centuries of weathering. Those who knew the road slowed to a crawl, and shambled over them with respect, the unwary from the cities hit them at speed, and banged their heads on their car roofs at the first bound. Strangers, hearing they were Roman, assumed they had been carefully preserved for archaeological purposes. The truth was that in Middlehope things survived; no one preserved them. They had always been there, and were still serviceable, why move them?

From under the Lawley to the upper reaches of the Teme valley is not so far, and perhaps the Devil will forgive the removal of his handiwork. It fits very suitably into the elusive world of Middlehope.

In *Never Pick up Hitch-Hikers* I even fired a few shots, tongue-in-cheek, at the concept of the New Town, and the painful process of incorporating four or five independent and probably reluctant settlements into an artificial whole.

Change is inescapable. But in fact there is nothing new about New Towns. Planned boroughs were set up hopefully in the Middle Ages, the grids of their neatly-laid-out streets can be seen plainly in aerial views. Some of them, like Ludlow, went from strength to strength. Some, like the shadowy plan in the ground levels of New Radnor, show where the failures withered away. Man never gives up the effort to alter his environment, to make his mark, good or bad, on the world around him.

'God gave all men all earth to love,' said Kipling, and over the years I have found my heart quite large enough to feel the truth of it. But loving Venice, Prague, Kashmir, Cape Comorin, or Falzeben, at the back of beyond above Merano, these belong among the Sunday treats, to be visited, marvelled at, enjoyed and remembered, graces to ornament and vary the basic stability of a weekday life, the spinal cord that binds everything together, the place where I live, work, and co-ordinate all experiences into a personal reconciliation, which is the point of living.

So Shropshire will be found, some evanescent glimpse, some oblique reflection of it, in everything I have written, and everything I shall write in the future, and I suspect I have left a faint trace of it everywhere I have been.

Floreat Salopia! I'm glad I was born here.

FURTHER READING

Anderson, John Corbet, *Shropshire: Its Early History and Antiquities*, Wilks and Southeran, 19–.

Owen & Blakeway, *History of Shrewsbury*, Harding, Lepard & Co., 1825.

Pevsner, Nikolaus, *Shropshire*, 'The Buildings of England' series, Penguin, 1958.

Randall, John, *History of Madeley*, 1880, Shropshire County Library, 19–.

Rees, Una (trans. and ed.), *The Cartulary of Shrewsbury Abbey*, 2 vols., National Library of Wales, Aberystwyth, 1975.

Rowley, Trevor, *The Shropshire Landscape*, Hodder & Stoughton, London, 1972.

INDEX

Index

Index